ATTEND TO STORIES

How to Flourish in Ministry

Karen D. Scheib

Attend to Stories: How to Flourish in Ministry

The General Board of Higher Education and Ministry leads and serves The United Methodist Church in the recruitment, preparation, nurture, education, and support of Christian leaders—lay and clergy—for the work of making disciples of Jesus Christ for the transformation of the world. The General Board of Higher Education and Ministry of The United Methodist Church serves as an advocate for the intellectual life of the church. The Board's mission embodies the Wesleyan tradition of commitment to the education of laypersons and ordained persons by providing access to higher education for all persons.

Wesley's Foundery Books is named for the abandoned foundery that early followers of John Wesley transformed into a church, which became the cradle of London's Methodist movement.

Attend to Stories: How to Flourish in Ministry

Copyright 2018 by Wesley's Foundery Books

Wesley's Foundery Books is an imprint of the General Board of Higher Education and Ministry, The United Methodist Church. All rights reserved.

Scriptures marked NRSV are from New Revised Standard Version Bible, copyright ©1989, National Council of the Churches of Christ in the United States of America. Used by permission. All rights reserved worldwide.

Scriptures marked NIV are taken from the Holy Bible, New International Version®, NIV® Copyright ©1973, 1978, 1984, 2011 by Biblica, Inc.™ Used by permission of Zondervan. All rights reserved worldwide. www.zondervan.com. The "NIV" and "New International Version" are trademarks registered in the United States Patent and Trademark Office by Biblica, Inc.™

Scriptures marked NLT are taken from the Holy Bible, New Living Translation, Copyright ©1996, 2004, 2007, 2013, 2015, by Tyndale House Foundation. Used by permission of Tyndale House Publishers Inc., Carol Stream, Illinois 60188. All rights reserved.

Scriptures marked NKJV are taken from the New King James Version®. Copyright © 1982 by Thomas Nelson. Used by permission. All rights reserved.

No part of this book may be reproduced in any form whatsoever, print or electronic, without written permission, except in the case of brief quotations embodied in critical articles or reviews. For information regarding rights and permissions, contact the Publisher, General Board of Higher Education and Ministry, PO Box 340007, Nashville, TN 37203-0007; phone 615-340-7393; fax 615-340-7048. Visit our website at www.gbhem.org.

All web addresses were correct and operational at the time of publication.

ISBN 978-1-945935-14-5

18 19 20 21 22 23 24 25 26 27—10 9 8 7 6 5 4 3 2 1

Manufactured in the United States of America

Contents

Preface | v

1. **Story Care: Attending to Stories of Personal and Pastoral Identity** | 1
   Story-Shaped Lives | 2
   Narrative Environments and Master Narratives | 6
   Attending to Life Stories | 8
   Intersecting Narratives: My Story | 11
   Story Care: Reprise | 15

2. **Learning to Read Ministry Stories** | 17
   A Close Reading of Two Pastoral Memoirs | 19

3. **Restorying: Challenging and Revising Unsustainable Narratives** | 39
   Restorying Unsustainable Personal Narratives | 40
   Reflections on Restorying Unsustainable Personal Narratives | 45
   Master Narratives of Success in Unsustainable Pastoral Narratives | 47
   Master Narratives of Clergy Health and Wellness | 51
   A Story of Clergy Health: The Medical Model | 53
   Challenging the Power of Master Narratives | 61

4. **A Christian Vision of Flourishing** | 65
   Visions of Flourishing | 67
   Reclaiming a Theological Vision of Flourishing in This Life | 71

CONTENTS

Flourishing Defined (Reprise) | 88

5. **Practices for Flourishing | 91**
   Practicing Love: The General Rules | 94
   Playing by (with) the General Rules | 102
   Honoring the Body: Preserving Health Through
      Preventative Care | 114
   Expanding Our Spiritual Practices | 117

6. **Writing as Spiritual Practice and Story Care | 119**
   Writing as a Spiritual Practice | 122
   Writing as a Healing Practice | 126
   How to Begin Writing as a Spiritual Practice | 136
   Writing and Story Care | 140
   Story Care and Pastoral Identity (Reprise) | 144

Preface

The ideas developed in this book emerged from a series of lectures I gave to the Georgia Pastor's School in the summer of 2016 on clergy self-care. At the time of the lecture, I had unease about the term *self-care*, and still do today. While I believe the intent of clergy self-care is to improve the flourishing of clergy, discussions of self-care have often been focused on describing the symptoms of ill health among clergy in order to improve physical health. I also worry that the term *self-care* places success or failure of self-care on no one other than myself. Fortunately, the discussions about clergy health and self-care are being increasingly replaced by a more holistic focus on clergy well-being and flourishing.

This book is a contribution to the emerging literature on clergy flourishing. In the first three chapters, I examine how our personal stories, including our stories of pastoral identity, can thwart or foster our flourishing in ministry. I propose a practice of story care through which we attend to our stories and revise them as needed to move toward greater well-being. The fourth chapter provides an outline of my understanding of a Christian vision of flourishing. The fifth chapter examines spiritual practices that can contribute to our flourishing, offering a creative adaptation of John Wesley's General Rules, which were developed to assist in the spiritual formation of those in the early Methodist movement. The final chapter considers how writing can be a spiritual practice fostering

PREFACE

closer attention to our stories as they develop, allowing us to revise those that undermine our well-being.

Many people contributed to my thinking in the process of bringing this book into being, and I am deeply appreciative of their contributions. Rev. Millie Kim and the directors of the Georgia Pastors School issued the invitation to think about clergy flourishing. Several research assistants provided assistance along the way: Jemiriye Fakunle, Abby Norman, and Lacey Hudspeth. Several current and former colleagues contributed ideas and comments on the text that enriched my thinking: E. Brooks Holifield, Roberta Bondi, Jonathan Strom, Tom Elliott, Ellen Shepard, and Bishop Larry Goodpaster. Ulrike Guthrie provided invaluable assistance as a developmental editor, and I am indebted to Dean Jan Love for making this assistance possible. Carmen Toussaint and those who have made Rivendell Writer's Colony possible provided the quiet space needed to finish this book. Kathy Armistead, publisher of Wesley's Foundery Books, saw the potential value in the book and is responsible for bringing it to you, and for that I am most grateful.

1
Story Care
Attending to Stories of Personal and Pastoral Identity

Most of us enter ministry in response to some sense of calling. We may feel called to serve God through caring for others, to a particular ministry of the local church, or more broadly to a life lived with careful attention to the movement of the Spirit. For some, an experience of call can be similar to their first conscious decision to dedicate their life to Christ—a distinctive event in which they recall with clarity the exact day, and perhaps even the hour and location. For others, a sense of call emerges gradually over time, an extension of their baptismal covenant that may be perceived first by family members, church members, and mentors who point out gifts and graces suited to ordained ministry. Call stories may lead us into various forms of ministry, ordained or not, sometimes in the church and sometimes beyond it. As diverse as call stories can be, they share a common conviction that the call to ministry is from God.

If your call leads you into ordained ministry, one thing becomes clear as you pursue official steps in the ordination process: to convince others that you are called to ministry you'd better have a good story. Candidates for ministry soon learn what counts as a good or acceptable call story and what does not. Once articulated, these call stories are often repeated for seminary admissions teams, congregational committees, ordination committees, and denominational officials. I suspect that once a candidate is ordained, these stories continue to serve as the foundation of one's expectations about the practice of ministry. And indeed, stories that once served an important function in setting a vocational path may continue to serve a person well, particularly if examined and revised amid an unfolding ministry. However, at times our call stories support assumptions about the nature of ministry and expectations of our role that undermine our well-being, as well as the faithfulness of both ourselves and those we serve. It is those stories—and how we can revise or restory them to remain true and helpful—that particularly interest me here.

Yet our call stories are also a part of our personal story. In this chapter I explore the formation and intersection of personal and pastoral identity through story. Our stories of pastoral identity and our understanding of ministry shape our practice of ministry in ways we may not realize. The process of intentionally reviewing our stories of call and identity over the course of our ministries and lives is what I call *story care*. This ongoing practice of story care can foster the formation of sustaining stories that contribute to our flourishing as we tend to the spiritual growth and well-being of those we serve, and it can help to root out stories that no longer make sense or have become skewed in some way.

Story-Shaped Lives

Stories are powerful, shaping our identity, and in turn, our behavior. But you already know that; you already practice that, for much of our time in ministry is spent listening to the stories of others. We are story-shaped beings with story-shaped lives, and we communicate who we are through the stories we tell. "If you want to know me," says narrative psychologist Dan McAdams, "then you must know my story, for my story defines who I am. And if I want to know myself, to gain insight into the meaning of my own life, then I, too, must come to know my own stories."[1] More than that: "Though I may think of myself as having a life story, I *am* my story."[2] Our very identity is composed by and communicated through story. Stories do many things, but their primary purpose is to convey meaning, including assigning meaning to the many practices in which we engage, from how we parent and eat to how we exercise and minister.

Narrative Identity and the Development of a Life Story

Our life story or life narrative is the "larger framework that provides a more or less cohesive, thematic organization of the multiple stories we have lived in the past, are living in the present, or imagine we may live in the future."[3] To say that we not only "*have* a life story, but that we *are* stories" is to claim that we live our lives "from a story perspective."[4] Our life stories, which include thoughts, feelings, and actions and can be communicated both verbally and nonverbally, are formed within the important

---

1 Dan P. McAdams, *The Stories We Live By: Personal Myths and the Making of the Self* (New York: Guilford Press, 1993), 11.
2 Karen D. Scheib, *Pastoral Care: Telling the Stories of Our Lives* (Nashville: Abingdon Press, 2016), 8. See also McAdams, *The Stories We Live By*, 5; and Gary M. Kenyon and William L. Randall, *Restorying Our Lives: Personal Growth Through Autobiographical Reflection* (Westport, CT: Praeger, 1997), 1.
3 Scheib, 6.
4 Kenyon and Randall, *Restorying Our Lives,* 15.

relationships and various contexts in which our lives unfold.[5] Our life stories have multiple strands composed of both internal, or "inside-out," and external, or "outside-in stories."[6] Our internal stories are those of our private internal world, which we communicate to others through our words and our actions.[7] External stories originate outside of us and include others' perceptions of and responses to us.[8] We then internalize these external stories and they become a part of our internal story.[9] When we are perceived by others through loving eyes, these external stories contribute to a sense of ourselves as loved. But when these external stories reflect less-positive perceptions or don't match our internal experience of ourselves, they may have a negative impact on our sense of self, inhibiting our ability to affirm certain aspects of ourselves.

We begin forming the stories of our lives in childhood as we absorb stories told in our families, read to us at bedtime, heard in church. Perhaps your family tells a familiar story at gatherings or reunions. Maybe it's about the time your father got pulled over for speeding but didn't notice the police car behind him until the siren broke through the raucous singing going on in the car.[10] Such stories communicate a sense of what it means to be a part of a particular family. We carry a virtual library of stories within us.[11] Do you still remember the stories you loved as a child? One of my favorites was *The Little Engine That Could*.[12] While riding my bike up

---

5   Kenyon and Randall, 15.
6   Kenyon and Randall, 34–35.
7   Kenyon and Randall, 34.
8   Kenyon and Randall, 35.
9   Kenyon and Randall, 35.
10 This story is from my own family history.
11 Kenyon and Randall, *Restorying Our Lives*, 38–39.
12 Watty Piper, *The Little Engine That Could*, 3rd print ed. (New York: Grosset & Dunlap, 2009). Originally published in 1930 by Platt & Munk, https://en.wikipedia.org/wiki/The_Little_Engine_That_Could, accessed August 8, 2017.

a steep hill to get to school, I'd say to myself, "I think I can, I think I can," just as the little train in the story did as she chugged up a big hill, confounding her skeptics.[13]

We draw on this trove of stories we begin collecting in childhood as we begin to engage self-consciously in constructing our life stories as adolescents. It is during this time in our lives that we begin to ask ourselves, "Who am I—as distinct from my parents?"[14] One's *"narrative identity"* is his or her "internalized and evolving story," constructed "consciously and unconsciously," which holds "together different aspects of the self."[15] For example, I may be very good at school, praised by my teachers, and held in esteem by good friends, but at home I'm still seen as the "baby" of the family and not expected to contribute much to conversations. We bring together multiple story strands to construct a personal narrative, which provides a coherent sense of self.

As we age and accumulate life experiences, our stories become thicker and more complex.[16] One or more central themes may emerge to organize our stories, providing continuity in the midst of change. Core themes in our life stories are often shaped by significant events, especially in our childhood—such as my notion that I am frail, or that, if I am the "baby" of the family, no one expects much of me (except to be cute and inept). Such themes may then serve as lenses through which new experiences are interpreted and incorporated into our evolving narrative identities and life stories. In my case, it could have made me continue to rely on others and simply be a cute, frail, needy person rather than exploring other possible identities for myself that might have been more true.

---

13 Piper.
14 McAdams, *The Stories We Live By*, 78.
15 Dan P. McAdams, *The Person: A New Introduction to Personality Psychology*, 4th ed. (New York: Wiley, 2006), 405.
16 Kenyon and Randall, *Restorying Our Lives*, 61.

CHAPTER 1

Whether you are aware of it or not, every time you share a story, even an anecdote or a snippet or a Facebook post or Like, you share something of who you are. Let's take a minute for an exercise to reflect on the connection between identity and life story.

Exercise

Throughout this text you will find a number of writing exercises, designed to help you practice intentionally expressing and reflecting on your stories of personal and pastoral identity.

1) Think about a specific story you often share about yourself when meeting someone for the first time. It doesn't have to be a long story. Maybe it is only a snippet, but something that communicates who you are. It may be where you are from, what you do, a favorite hobby, something about your name, or something quite unique to you. (Jot down your answer.)

2) Now reflect on how the story you chose communicates something about your identity. What do you hope people think about you when they learn this story snippet? What are you conveying by telling it? Write down an insight you gained about yourself from attending to this story.

Narrative Environments and Master Narratives

We collect the stories for our internal libraries from the various "narrative environments," or the contexts in which we live.[17] Narrative environments are any "context in which we talk about our lives" to others or to ourselves.[18] Each narrative environment contains a vast "collection of written and oral narratives" in all the various forms you can imagine: movies, TV shows, books, gossiping,

---

17   Kenyon and Randall, 50.
18   Kenyon and Randall, 50..

Facebook posts, and even the micro-fiction of Twitter posts.[19] We are not always aware of the role of these stories or the extent to which they shape our stories.

Narrative environments influence our stories in several ways. First are the rules of storytelling determined in narrative environments: who can tell which stories, which stories are considered appropriate in what context, whose voices are heard, and also whose voices are silenced. The rules of storytelling can limit which stories we feel free to tell. For example, a woman raised in a faith tradition that does not allow women's ordination may feel a call to ministry but fear being judged or silenced if she tells her call story. Second, "master narratives" embedded in narrative environments communicate beliefs and values about the world.[20] Master narratives are usually about grand topics, such as race, money, ambition, gender, sexuality, justice, and religion, all of which have an impact on our identity.[21]

Much of the time, however, we are not aware of the influence of these narrative environments. We simply accept as valid the view of the world conveyed by a particular environment, as reality, as simply the way it is. Consequently, I see women students from traditions in which women are not allowed to preach enter a required preaching class at my seminary with great trepidation. However, by exposing ourselves like this to a new narrative environment with a new set of rules and stories, we can learn to question and resist the limits imposed by the stories from the original environment. I have seen some of the aforementioned women students who were convinced they were not or could not be

---

19 William R. Randall and Elizabeth McKim, *Reading Our Lives: The Poetics of Growing Old* (New York: Oxford Univeristy Press, 2008), 50.
20 Randall and McKim, 52.
21 Randall and McKim, 52.

"preachers" discover a powerful prophetic preaching voice once they let go of the old or original story of not being permitted and called to preach and instead embraced their alternative story of being capable preachers.

Exercise

Take a few moments to reflect on a story from childhood that is important to you. How did this story reflect the values of the narrative environments of your family and culture? What values and master narratives about gender roles, race, or autonomy and community are embedded in this story? Do you see yourself still shaped by these values? How have these master narratives shaped your sense of identity in positive ways or constrained who you can be in order to feel accepted in the larger culture?

Attending to Life Stories

Most of the time we are so caught up in simply living our life stories that we are scarcely aware of our role as authors, as creators, as shapers of those stories. We can choose to revise and reinterpret the stories we have created or that have been created for us and about us. Revising them can reshape us—in my case, from a "frail," withdrawn child to a competent public preacher and professor—for we may be unaware of the power that these stories hold over us: how they hold us back, or how they prevent us from exploring particular talents or aspects of ourselves and of the world.

The stories we tell about our ministry are important and worthy of our attention because they shape our practice of ministry. Periodically it's useful to ask ourselves, "Do my stories of ministry and care, which are part of my larger life stories, move me toward flourishing or thwart my flourishing?" To flourish is to grow well, to be healthy, or "to grow luxuriantly."[22] The abundant life, which Jesus promised us in John 10:10 as a vision of flourishing, is a life lived in love.

There are many things that can hamper our growth in love and thwart our flourishing, including the stories we carry about ourselves. To move toward abundant life requires letting go of stories that don't foster flourishing and discovering alternative stories that do. Stories that thwart flourishing tell us we are not good enough, or we must earn love, or it is our job to meet everyone else's needs.

The events of our lives and the past that has shaped us can't be undone. We can, however, reinterpret past events and assign new meanings to them—life-giving meanings. We can also bring other neglected stories to the fore. Through the process of restorying,[23] we can revise the interpretations we have assigned to our stories, including those stories that define who we are and how we care for others and ourselves.

Learning to Read Our Life Stories

While we may not reflect consciously on our life stories, when we are able to see our lives as stories and have enough distance to assess them, we become aware that our stories are continually unfolding.[24] Often when we go back and recall a life story from an earlier time, we are actually reinterpreting it as much as we are recalling it. We can't help but read the past through the present. For example, for many years I thought of receiving a call to ministry in my early twenties as something unprecedented and unexpected. Even though I was quite involved with my local church, I did

---

22 Merriam-Webster.com, s.v. "true," accessed January 8, 2018, https://www.merriam-webster.com/dictionary/flourish.
23 Kenyon and Randall, *Restorying Our Lives*, 1.
24 Kenyon and Randall, viii.

not consider ordained ministry an option since I did not know any women ministers. At that point in my life, I was trying to decide on a vocational direction and had imagined a medically related profession. When I did experience a call to ministry, I was surprised, even though I had really enjoyed my service to the church.

We may think our call stories have not changed over time, but our interpretations of the stories probably have changed. Such reinterpretation is almost inevitable since we view our past experience from our present vantage point. I think I remember exactly what it was like to receive my call, but from the vantage point of almost forty years later, I recognize that the story has been revised over time.

Now when I look back, I can see inklings of a developing call that I did not see earlier. When I was in high school, I was the chaplain for our local chapter of Job's Daughters, a philanthropic organization with a name drawn from the book of Job. Most girls aspired to be elected queen, which was the most important leadership position, but I wanted to be the chaplain. The chaplain was the one who got to lead the prayers, kneeling at the altar. I held this position long enough ago that I can't quite remember the exact year, but I think I was a senior in high school, well before I considered entering the ministry or had any sense of call. I do remember that when I took on this role, my mother had been hospitalized for the first time due to a serious flare-up of her multiple sclerosis, which had been diagnosed just a few years before. The idea of kneeling quietly at the altar and publicly leading prayers appealed to me at a tumultuous time in my life. Now when I look back at my call to ministry, I wonder if my desire to be the chaplain was a foreshadowing of what was yet to come.

Exercise

Think back on a story about yourself that you have had for a long time. Has the meaning of this story changed for you at all? Are there multiple ways to interpret it? What would it mean to interpret that story differently?

Intersecting Narratives: My Story

The preceding vignette gives a glimpse of how our call stories are intertwined with our personal stories, of who we are and who we are becoming. To further illumine the way our narratives of personal and pastoral identity intersect and influence each other, I'll share a bit more of my story.

My mother was diagnosed with multiple sclerosis (MS) in 1968, when she was thirty-six and I was fourteen. Though now I know she had the primary progressive type of MS, one of the more rare and devastating forms of the disease, all I knew then was that she had MS. Her health declined steadily over the ten years from her diagnosis to her death. She first lost the ability to walk. Shortly after, ataxia in her arms meant that any attempt at purposeful movement resulted in a wild flailing about. As you can imagine, this made lots of things difficult for her. No effective treatments were available at the time, and home health-care services were limited. While a visiting nurse came in occasionally and my grandmother eventually came to stay with us, much of the day-to-day care of the household and physical care of my mother fell to my father, my sister, and me. My mother spent the last five years of her life confined to her bed, which was a difficult period for all of us.

I returned to the church as a young adult, after having dropped out of confirmation class a few years before. I was struggling with the realities of illness and death and looking for answers to big questions. While I found a supportive community in the church, I also found beliefs about care that easily reinforced those I had developed in caring for my mother, such as the belief that caring for others always comes first. The form of the Great Commandment that stuck with me was this: love God first, others second, yourself third. Now I am pretty sure that the biblical text does not place love of God, self, and other in a hierarchal arrangement. I already had a template for a story that told me caring for myself could put others, specifically my mother, at risk. If I wanted to save her, and of course I did, I had to sacrifice my own growth, my own desires. I was not aware of thinking this at the time; it operated mostly outside of my awareness, but I lived out of this story. At some deep level, I hoped I could stave off her death by taking good enough care of her. I equated caring *for* her with taking care *of* her.

My mother died in January 1979, during my second year in seminary. I dealt with my loss by losing myself in my work and earned some of the best grades of my seminary career. Six months later, I was ordained a deacon in The United Methodist Church.[25] In addition to losing myself in work, I also dealt with her death by finding someone else to take care of, and nine months after her death, I married the man I had been dating off and on for a year. I don't recommend marriage as the best way to deal with grief.

When I was ordained an elder in The United Methodist Church in 1982, I had been in ministry two years and married for three.[26] I began my first appointment serving as an associate pastor in June 1980 with Rev. Bert Lewis, the senior pastor, at St. Mark's United Methodist Church in San Diego. Two days after I was ordained at

---

25 At this time the United Methodist church had a two-step ordination process in which one was ordained a deacon and became a probationary member of the Annual Conference until becoming ordained an elder and a member in full connection.

26 In The United Methodist Church, ordination services occur during the yearly meeting of the Annual Conference, rather than in the local church in which one is serving, as in some denominations.

the close of the Annual Conference, the bishop called up Reverend Lewis to thank him for his term of service as the Conference secretary, an important and esteemed position. The bishop commended Reverend Jones for his faithful and dedicated service, and for working "twelve, fourteen, eighteen hours a day."[27] And I clearly remember thinking, *Oh no! This is the model I am expected to follow!* Of course, I interpreted the bishop's words through my own life story. I tucked this vignette away alongside other stories from my family and the larger culture about the importance of hard work, responsibility, being a good girl, and taking care of others. Working hard, putting Jesus first, others second, and myself third—a story I had learned in church—became an unquestioned part of my life story.

As I look back on this now, many years later, I am quite convinced that my mother's illness was a significant factor in forming my call to ministry. In the later stages of her illness, my mother could not feed herself and it was my job, along with my sister, to do so. What I took from this experience as a teenager was that caring for another was a life-or-death matter. As a young adult, I carried this assumption about caring into my ministry practice. Though it fueled a zeal for ministry, it was detrimental to my own well-being. I do think it is inevitable that our stories of call and ministry are shaped in the narrative environments of family and church. The particular way my personal and family stories intersected with my story of call and ministry led to an unsustainable story and eventually my departure from parish ministry.

The narrative environments of culture and generation also played a role in shaping my narratives of personal and pastoral identity. I am a baby boomer, born in 1954, raised in a white family

---

27 This is not a direct quotation, but rather my own recollection of the events of that day.

in California, a family moving from working-class to middle-class status. My mother was a high school graduate, something her father had not achieved. My father was the first one in his family to receive a college diploma. I was a child in the 1950s, raised to be a "good girl," to be "seen and not heard." The cultural messages of the 1950s also shaped my notions of what it meant for me as a woman to care for others and for myself.

My life story and my story of becoming a pastor intersected in unhelpful ways. I went straight from college to seminary and into the local church, where I served six years before a personal crisis led me to leave local church ministry to pursue doctoral work. Unfortunately, I had still not examined or changed the assumptions about the patterns of caregiving that were still problematic for me. That did not occur until sometime later.

Becoming aware of the impact of parts of our life stories that do not move us toward flourishing is rarely easy. But it is the first step to making a change. For me, this process has required therapy, writing as a spiritual practice, compassionate friends, and significantly revising my life story. Attending to and revising our stories about care will lead to new theological and psychological insights, a renewed sense of self as a person, and greater joy in vocation as pastors and teachers.

Exercise

1) Think of an experience of either giving or receiving care as a child or adolescent. Jot down the image or story that comes to your mind.

2) What did you learn about caring for others and yourself from this experience? Is this a story that comes to mind often when you think of the meaning of care? What do you find helpful about what you learned about care from this experience? How are

the lessons you learned about care evident in your ministry? What lessons are no longer helpful to you?

Story Care: Reprise

Caring for ourselves requires attending to the stories of our lives. We not only have stories; we *are* our stories. Much of the time, however, we are so caught up living our life stories that we are scarcely aware of our role as authors of our own stories. When we are finally able to see our lives as continuously unfolding stories, we can accept the integrity and uniqueness of our life stories and claim the power to revise and reinterpret the stories we have created or that have been created for us.[28]

The practice of *story care* is a form of self-care, which is applicable to our own life stories as well as others'. As a form of pastoral care, the purpose of story care is to generate stories that promote growth in love of God, others, and self and flourishing in God's abundant grace.[29] A close reading of life stories allows us to perceive God's presence in human stories, and discern those that move us toward or interfere with growth in love. Whatever your situation, I am convinced that paying deep attention to our life stories is beneficial. Such story care leads to psychological and spiritual growth, and significant transformation of our life stories.

---

[28] Kenyon and Randall, *Restorying Our Lives*, viii.
[29] Karen Scheib, *Pastoral Care*, 4–5.

2

Learning to Read Ministry Stories

The goal of story care is to discern which stories give life and foster flourishing as God intends and which stories leave us languishing. Story care means paying attention to how our stories become formed, indeed, how we are actively constructing our life stories. While we can't change the past events of our lives, the interpretations we give to these events can and do change. At times, we may find ourselves in a story that no longer seems to fit who we are, such as the "good girl," or the "star athlete," or the "frail one." Sometimes we find ourselves in a context or narrative environment that pushes us to conform to a story that doesn't fit who we truly are. Learning to read our stories more closely is the first step in discerning which stories are life-giving and move us toward flourishing and which stories leave us languishing and must be revised or let go.

Improving our ability to read a written story can improve our ability to read life stories.[1] In this chapter, we're going to practice

---

1   Scheib, *Pastoral Care*, 102 (see chap. 1, n. 2).

reading life stories both by looking at some pastoral memoirs, and by "reading" our own life stories closely along the way.

If you learned to do biblical exegesis in seminary or through serious Bible study, you already have the basic skills you need to practice the art of close reading. To perform an exegesis simply means "to relate in detail or expound."[2] Any time we dig deeper into a written text to decipher its meaning, whether a scripture passage, a poem, or a newspaper editorial, we engage in the process of close reading.[3] As we exegete a text, we ask questions of it: What's the larger story or backstory here? What is the context or setting of the story? Who are the main characters? What are the narrative environments or master narratives that may be influencing the action of the characters? Is there a central conflict? Is the storyteller constrained in how he or she tells his or her story? Are parts of the story under-told or left untold?

You may not have thought about extending this skill to reading—or exegeting—life stories. But you do just that when listening to a church member who has come to you for counseling or a friend who unburdens himself to you. Imagine you are visiting Jane, a member of your congregation, who is facing her first colonoscopy. As you talk with Jane, you wonder whether her anxiety is out of proportion for this routine procedure. You become curious about what's behind her anxiety. As you begin to ask questions, you realize that she has *confined* the story of what will happen in the surgery, anticipating a negative outcome. You also realize there is a *backstory* you have never heard, which is shaping her story. While you already knew that her father died when she was a teenager, you did not know he had died of colon cancer, or how difficult

---

2   John Hayes and Carl Holladay, *Biblical Exegesis: A Beginners Handbook,* 3rd ed. (Louisville: Westminster John Knox Press, 2007), 1.
3   Hayes and Holladay, 1.

this experience was for Jane. As Jane now says, "I rarely talk about this time in my life with anyone—it is too painful," you begin to sense how her *under-told* and *untold stories* may be shaping her current story of anxiety about a normally routine procedure. As you listen closely, you are practicing a close reading of her story. As you engage in conversation, sharing your curiosity, Jane is able to expand and deepen her story, allowing for new interpretations of past events, which also allows different possible outcomes. You have just provided story care for Jane.

A Close Reading of Two Pastoral Memoirs

One of the ways to practice and improve our ability to read life stories, our own or another's, is through a close reading or exegesis of a memoir. An old adage says, "Tell me your story and I'll find mine." Through reading another's story we may gain a little distance and a new perspective on our stories, seeing things we missed before. Exegeting another person's life story may feel a bit easier than trying to read our own stories closely while we are in the midst of living them. By practicing the skills of life story exegesis on memoirs, we can strengthen our ability to read our life stories in the midst of their unfolding. Memoirs work well because they present a portion of a life story rather than a full autobiography. Pastoral memoirs can be particularly helpful as we sort out our own stories of call and pastoral identity to discern whether these are sustaining or draining.

We are going to look at two recent examples of pastoral memoirs, though this genre has a long history.[4] In *Leaving Church: A*

---

4   See, for example, Augustine's *Confessions,* or John Wesley's *Journals.* Examples of longer pastoral autobiographies include those of Martin Luther King Jr., Thomas Merton, and Howard Thurman.

CHAPTER 2

Memoir of Faith, Barbara Brown Taylor tells her story of moving into and out of local church ministry.[5] Eugene H. Peterson reflects retrospectively on his process of forming a pastoral identity in *The Pastor: A Memoir.*[6] I have chosen these memoirs because they both deal with the formation of pastoral identity—that part of our personal identity related to our role in ministry, ordained or not.

In our close reading of these memoirs, I focus on three story strands frequently found in narratives of pastoral identity formation, which were named in the pastoral vignette with Jane. While these story strands can be identified through the kinds of questions we ask in the process of life story exegesis, they are not the only strands we might identify, nor do they provide an exhaustive analysis of these memoirs or our own life narratives.[7] In our practice of close reading, we will focus on the following story strands: (1) *Confining stories* limit our identity in some way and may be unable to sustain us in difficult times. Some form of conflict, either internal or external, may underlie these stories. (2) *Backstories* reflect the influence of the narrative environments and master narratives communicated through family and culture. They also reflect the larger historical context and setting of the story. (3) *Under-told or untold stories* are parts of the story that seem missing or are not fully developed. These three elements are present to differing degrees in the two memoirs we will examine.

Barbara Brown Taylor: Finding and Leaving Church

In *Leaving Church*, Barbara Brown Taylor tells the story of her entrance into and exit from parish ministry. Her title is a

---

5   Barbara Brown Taylor, *Leaving Church: A Memoir of Faith* (New York: HarperCollins, 2007).
6   Eugene H. Peterson, *The Pastor: A Memoir* (New York: HarperCollins, 2011).
7   See Scheib, *Pastoral Care,* for a full presentation of life story exegesis.

provocative one, but also a bit misleading. Though Brown Taylor does tell us about leaving the pulpit of a *particular church,* she does not abandon the church. Rather, she finds she has to redefine her relationship to the church, her understanding of ministry, and the practices that sustain her. The most important message of the book is Brown Taylor's discovery that the stories she carried about work of the ministry did not allow her to be faithful and whole. I suspect it was only in retrospect, while writing her memoir, that Brown Taylor realized how her stories of ministry confined and ultimately failed her. My purpose in sharing her story is to encourage a closer look at the stories we carry about ourselves in ministry. Do your stories promote your well-being as well as that of the church? Do your stories allow you to be both faithful and whole?

A Confining Story

In the first few pages of Brown Taylor's memoir, we get a glimpse of what led her to leave the pulpit of the small country church she once thought of as her dream church. While walking around a city block one evening, the fragrance of honeysuckle stirs a realization that she has lost track of the world around her.[8] As she wonders how this happened, she realizes that she believed taking time for herself "felt like a betrayal of divine trust."[9] As a priest, her responsibility to care for others took precedence over noticing her own needs.[10] Her narrative of ministry confined her ability to fully attend her own needs, despite her efforts at self-care, which included exercise, counseling, and vacations.[11] Even though she

---

8 Brown Taylor, *Leaving Church*, 4.
9 Brown Taylor, 5.
10 Brown Taylor, 5.
11 Brown Taylor, 6.

knew she was depleting herself, she felt that if she gave herself fully to God's work, "God would keep me in business."[12] Underlying this confining narrative is a conflict between her commitment to care for others and the need to care for herself.

She followed the conventional advice for self-care, but it was not enough. The confining story she held about ministry undermined her efforts at self-care. She imagined moving out to the country to a smaller congregation, anticipating that the demands of ministry would lessen.[13] Still, she took with her a view of ministry in which it was her job to feed others.[14] When she decided to leave Christ Calvary in the midst of congregational conflict over building a larger sanctuary to accommodate the church's growth, she realized that feeding others was no longer feeding her.[15] The decision to leave was not an easy one. She confesses, "I had resigned with a mortgaged heart and a sense of defeat so great that I had no ready answer for friends who asked me why I left."[16] Toward the end of the book, as she reflects further on what led her to leave, she realizes that her desire to be good by doing good had diminished her and left her feeling less than whole.[17]

While Brown Taylor does not talk explicitly about the formation of her pastoral identity, this process is evident through her memoir. Brown Taylor tells us that her desire to help others was the primary reason she pursued ordination. In fact, she believed that helping others was her essential purpose in life.[18] She looked to Jesus as her example of ministry, seeing someone who was "always feeding

---

12 Brown Taylor, 6.
13 Brown Taylor, 6.
14 Brown Taylor, 75.
15 Brown Taylor, 113.
16 Brown Taylor, 126.
17 Brown Taylor, 127.
18 Brown Taylor, 47.

people, healing people, teaching people, and helping people."[19] Though she tried to "serve Christ in all persons" she got to the point where she didn't really want to do it anymore.[20] Perhaps without knowing it, rather than serving Christ in others, she was trying to be Christ, to be the one generating food for the five thousand, rather than merely being one of the disciples who hands out the bread. Building her narrative of ministry on this model confined her narrative in ways that undermined her well-being.

My intention is not to be critical of Brown Taylor, who is not so different from many of us. Rather I want to draw attention to the impact that confining stories of ministry can have on our lives. Neither am I telling you Brown Taylor's story to advocate that you leave parish ministry. Rather, I see *Leaving Church* as a cautionary tale on how the confining stories we tell ourselves about how we are to go about ministry can impact our well-being. In my reading of Brown Taylor's memoir, it was not leaving church that saved her but the growing awareness that her way of doing ministry was not sustainable. Though she does not use the language of story, what I see her doing in her memoir is reviewing, reinterpreting, and revising her story. While we see the end of one story in *Leaving Church,* we *also* see the beginning of a new one. The decision to leave the church freed her to see herself and those with whom she worked differently. She begins to practice Sabbath in a genuine way that had previously eluded her. Because she is no longer telling herself the story that she has to take care of everyone else, she is beginning to take care of herself.

---

19 Brown Taylor, 47.
20 Brown Taylor, 113.

CHAPTER 2

Exercise

Identify the parts of Barbara Brown Taylor's story that resonate with your own experience. Then take a few minutes to write down a brief description of a time you have struggled to care for yourself in ministry. Can you pinpoint any confining stories that contributed to your experience of struggle?

Backstories

The various narrative environments in which we grow up have a significant influence on the development of our life stories. As Brown Taylor tells how she came into ministry, we discover that she was not raised in a Christian household and had little experience in church. She came back to the church as her religious experiments through high school and into college became more urgent in the midst of the escalation of the Vietnam War. Brown Taylor was born in 1951, square in the middle of the baby boom, and her identity took shape in the larger historical context of the 1960s: the Vietnam War, as well as the assassinations of two Kennedys and Martin Luther King Jr. Brown Taylor had witnessed all of these events by the time she was eighteen.[21] Like many of her generation, she was perhaps formed more significantly by events happening outside the church than within it. During her college years, she became committed to nonviolence and social justice.[22]

In this same time period, she encountered the theology of Bonhoeffer and Tillich and discovered a new and intriguing view of God she had not heard in church.[23] Wanting to know more and dig deeper, she enrolled in seminary.[24] While in seminary she

---

21 Brown Taylor, 27.
22 Brown Taylor, 27.
23 Brown Taylor, 27.
24 Brown Taylor, 22.

found her home in the Episcopal Church and was confirmed at the age of twenty-five just before graduation.[25] At that time, she had no intention of being ordained and was a bit wary of the whole business.[26] After serving for a year as a pastoral intern at a large church, she put her doubts aside and pursued full-time ministry and ordination.[27]

In many ways, Brown Taylor embodies many of the traits of the baby boomer generation: a strong work ethic, a deep spiritual hunger, a hopeful idealism, a desire to improve the world, a tendency toward perfectionism, and the proneness to evaluate options and make decisions based on internal standards.[28] We can see elements of these traits in her story, reminding us of the power of the narrative environments of historical location and her generation in shaping our pastoral identity and experience of ministry.

The narrative environment of a particular congregation can also influence our stories of ministry. No one in Brown Taylor's congregation seemed to challenge her expectations of herself or the exhausting pace she set. Her story reminds us that a congregation's expectations and narratives of ministry may unintentionally reinforce our own stories in unhelpful ways. In Brown Taylor's case, the conflict about expanding the church facilities can also be seen as an example of conflicting stories about what the church should be and become. This is the impasse that finally led Brown Taylor to question the pastoral identity she had formed.

---

25 Brown Taylor, 31.
26 Brown Taylor, 31.
27 Brown Taylor, 33, 35.
28 Jaco Hamman, *Becoming a Pastor: Forming Self and Soul for Ministry, Revised and Updated* (Cleveland: Pilgrim Press, 2014), 16, citing William Strauss and Neil Howe, *Generations: The History of America's Future, 1584 to 2069* (New York: Quill, 1991), 303.

Exercise

Jot down some of the backstories that reflect the influence of the narrative environments that have shaped your identity. For example, does your family tell a particular story frequently? What does this story tell about your family's identity? How does the generation you are a part of shape your personal and pastoral identity?

Untold Stories

Two additional kinds of story we look for in life story exegesis are those that are not fully told and those that are missing entirely. As I reread Brown Taylor's memoir, I was struck by an important part of the story that receives little attention: how she first came to be the pastor at Grace-Calvary. Brown Taylor discovered Grace-Calvary when she and her husband decided they wanted to move out of Atlanta and began looking around the north Georgia mountains for a place to live and an empty pulpit. After visiting Grace-Calvary, she declared to her husband, "I want this church."[29] The pulpit, however, was not empty, but filled by a well-loved pastor. Shortly after her visit to the church, she heard of the sudden death of the pastor. Worried about her covetousness, she waited three days to ask the bishop to put her name into consideration.[30] This is about all she tells us of the pastor's death.

An important part of the story is not fully told. She becomes the minister in charge after the sudden and unexpected death of a former beloved pastor. She does not tell us about the congregation's grief or how she shepherded them through this loss. How might the congregation's grief and her deep sense of compassion have exacerbated her inability to say no, to set limits, or to find other ways to feed her soul instead of caring for others? How

---

29 Brown Taylor, *Leaving Church*, 14.
30 Brown Taylor, 19.

might the congregants' unresolved grief have been linked to their fears of growth and leaving their familiar sanctuary? Brown Taylor reports that as she became more and more exhausted, she began to feel depressed and "upended by great waves of grief that caught me entirely off guard."[31] I can't help but wonder whether this grief was all her own, or whether she had somehow become the carrier for the congregation's unexpressed grief.

We don't know whether Brown Taylor simply left this part of the story out of her memoir, or whether the grief she and the congregation felt after the death of the former pastor simply went untold. What difference would it have made to her and the congregation had they been able to craft a story of their grief together? There is no guarantee that the church would still not have found itself years later in conflict over expansion, but they might not have found themselves at an impasse. We know that the consequences of unresolved grief in individuals can lead to depression, be expressed in anger, and lead to impaired health. I am convinced that the same is true for congregations, and if you look below the surface of many church conflicts, you will find unresolved grief.

A second part of the story that Brown Taylor leaves out is her experience of being the first woman minister at Grace-Calvary. Brown Taylor was ordained in 1983, just seven years after women were officially approved for ordination in the Episcopal Church. Perhaps she deemed that this part of her experience did not advance the story of her memoir. However, having served a small congregation as its first woman pastor around the same time that Brown Taylor was serving her church, I would argue that this part of her story is relevant to the pressure she felt to succeed and to meet the expectations of the congregation. Many of the women I know who served as the first woman pastor of a congregation

---

31 Brown Taylor, 101.

around that time felt the pressure to succeed not only for themselves but for all other women in ministry and for those wishing to enter it.

Exercise

Can you identify any under-told or untold stories in your own life that had an impact on your experience of ministry? Just try to name these for now, in writing, if you can. Acknowledging the presence and power of these stories can be painful. Be kind to yourself as you do this. In chapter 6 I'll introduce a method to reflect on these under-told and untold stories, so we'll return to your notes then.

Eugene Peterson: Forming a Countercultural Pastoral Identity

Eugene Peterson's story of his formation as a pastor is quite different from Brown Taylor's and gives us another perspective on pastoral identity formation. He tells a beautiful story of falling in love with ministry, including the ups and downs, and earthly struggles that accompany any real love story.[32] Like Brown Taylor, Peterson did not grow up thinking he would become a pastor.[33] In fact, the image he had of pastors from those he had known had left a rather bad impression. As we read Peterson's memoir closely, we will examine the same three story strands we identified in Brown Taylor's narrative, though in a slightly different order.

Backstory

Our families, as well as the places we grow up, are important narrative environments that influence the formation of our life stories. Peterson's family environment, the place he considers home, and the denomination in which he was raised play an important

---

32 Peterson, *The Pastor*, 2.
33 Peterson, 18.

role in forming his backstory. Peterson begins his memoir by telling us about the place that shaped him and to which he continually returns as a touch point while living in eighteen different homes and multiple states and countries over the course of his ministry.[34] His father bought property beside a lake in Montana in 1946 and began building the family home in 1948.[35] The sixteen-year-old Peterson helped with this construction project.[36] The Montana Peterson knew as a teenager was filled with mining and logging camps, one-room schoolhouses, and grange halls.[37]

Although Peterson was raised in a denomination wary of the ways of the world, he was steeped in Bible stories early on as he accompanied his mother, who taught Bible studies in logging camps around their Montana home.[38] He credits his early exposure to the Bible and his firm grounding in scripture for leading him to doctoral work in biblical studies.[39] He was training to be a biblical scholar when he found himself working part-time in a church in White Plains, New York, to support himself and his new wife. While teaching a class on Revelation and working as an associate pastor, he was drawn to John of Patmos, who then informed his experience of being a pastor and became his patron saint of pastors.[40]

Most of Peterson's ministry was spent in a church that he and his wife founded; it began by meeting in the basement of their home. He describes it as a church that did not look like a church, and it was soon known unofficially as the "church of the

---

34 Peterson, 14.
35 Peterson, 9–10.
36 Peterson, 10.
37 Peterson, 27.
38 Peterson, 28–29.
39 Peterson, 17.
40 Peterson, 21–22.

catacombs."[41] Peterson's church eventually outgrew its basement home, and he envisioned a new building in one of the new suburbs developing outside of Baltimore. Just as Peterson turned to scripture for the foundation of his pastoral identity, so too did he find inspiration in scripture for the kind of church he hoped to form. The book of Acts provided an image of the church that challenged the popular misconception that salvation is "God's business" and the "church is our business."[42] He came to realize, however, that it is all God's business.

An important dimension of Peterson's backstory is the generation of which he was a part, as well as the historical periods in which he grew up and was in active ministry. Peterson was born in 1932, and as a member of the "Silent Generation," grew up during the Great Depression. He became a pastor in the post–World War II boom of the 1950s. After some time as an associate pastor, he was called to build a church in the newly expanding suburbs of Baltimore in the early 1960s when many Christian churches were being planted, buoyed by postwar optimism and economic development. We also see a reflection of master stories shaping his ministry at this time. When Peterson talks about his fellow pastors, notice they are all men. Women had yet to enter ministry in any significant numbers in the 1960s.

Exercise

Jot down some of the ways that the generation of which you are a part, the time in which you grew up, and the place where you spent your formative years have influenced your personal and pastoral identity.

---

41 Peterson, 117.
42 Peterson, 117.

Confining Narratives

The confining narratives that Peterson pushes against were those he felt were imposed from the outside, rather than internal stories he carried (as was the case for Brown Taylor). In both instances, the narrative environments of family, church, and culture play a role in shaping pastoral identity. Peterson pushes against images of ministry and church that he finds neither life-giving nor consistent with his understanding of how God works in the world. One of the experiences that led to greater clarity about his pastoral role was the two years he spent in a group led by a psychiatrist and offered by a local psychiatric clinic, a group to improve clergy effectiveness in meeting the mental health needs of parishioners.[43] On Tuesday mornings, when he met with the psychiatrist and other pastors, he began seeing his church members in terms of their problems.[44] While he found this training helpful, he also discovered it was changing his perceptions of parishioners and of himself as a pastor. He realized that his primary role as a pastor was instead to assist his parishioners in their spiritual formation and see them through the lens of God's grace.[45]

Peterson discovered that forming a pastoral identity is not always easy. He wrote, "I couldn't help observing that there was a great deal of confusion and dissatisfaction all around me with pastoral identity." He noted that both pastors and congregations could easily become disillusioned with each other and looked for someone or something else.[46]

Peterson blamed some of this role confusion on leadership models from the realms of politics, business, and celebrity culture

---

43 Peterson, 132.
44 Peterson, 138.
45 Peterson, 140.
46 Peterson, 5.

being applied to ministry.[47] He argued that these models of leadership can be misleading for pastors and inconsistent with the Christian tradition. Peterson resisted these confining narratives of what pastoral leadership ought to look like. Instead, he drew on biblical stories and images to form his notion of a pastor as one who is attentive to the movement of God in people's lives here and now, asserting that the "kingdom of God . . . is primarily local, relentlessly personal, and prayerful without ceasing."[48] This way of being a pastor, said Peterson, is often not noticed, and it took him a while to claim his ministry as primarily shaped by a vision of the kingdom of God.

In order to resist the confining narratives about ministry that were popular at the time, Peterson turned to an unlikely model for ministry, John of Patmos. While teaching a course on the book of Revelation at a seminary, Peterson was also in his first pastorate. Peterson saw parallels between the world in which John of Patmos ministered and his own in New York City. In Peterson's view, New York reflected similar "pagan conditions" as those in Rome during John's ministry.[49] Peterson's study of John of Patmos broadened his imagination of what it meant to be a pastor and to participate in God's work of salvation.

Peterson's memoir shows that he has paid attention to his own stories. He weaves a pastoral identity from story threads of his childhood, experiences of marriage, the formation of a new congregation and the building of a church, the cultural context, and the daily rhythms of being a pastor. While he does not use the language of narrative environments, he has some awareness of how his identity as a pastor was shaped by his early family life, as well as the influence

---

47 Peterson, 5.
48 Peterson, 5.
49 Peterson, 20.

of cultural trends. We see him rejecting stories about ministry and church that he finds neither life-giving nor consistent with biblically informed views. Through his story, we *see* him becoming a pastor.

Exercise

Identify images or expectations about who and what a minister is or ought to be and write about how these have affected your process of pastoral identity formation or confined your story of pastoral identity. What are the sources of these images or expectations? What are some of the ways you resist the images or models of ministry that you find confining or contrary to your understanding of who you are called to be in ministry?

An Under-Told or Untold Story?

It can be difficult to identify the under-told or untold stories in a life narrative, whether our own or one in a memoir. In a memoir, an author limits the story to a set of events, a theme, or a certain time period, and may intentionally leave out what he or she deems not to be important to the story told in the memoir, or even events that author simply would rather not share. In our own life narratives, we are more likely to leave painful or shameful narratives untold or underdeveloped. We might also skim over stories we don't consider important or that we take for granted as simply being the way things were at the time. Other under-told stories might remain this way for fear that telling them will make us seem odd or different.

In Peterson's memoir, I find it more difficult to identify stories that are left *un*told than I did in Brown Taylor's. However, there is some evidence of stories that may be *under*-told. In the case of the story I examine, I suspect the story is under-told for two reasons: first, it may not have been essential to the way Peterson shaped

CHAPTER 2

his narrative; and second, it may have been that this story just reflected the way things were at the time and the story seemed unimportant. The story I consider under-told is the one of his wife, Jan, and her role in his ministry. Peterson does devote one chapter to her and mentions her throughout the book, so her story is not completely untold. Let's look at her story first, so we might determine if hers is an under-told story.

In the chapter titled "Jan," Peterson tells us how he met her and pursued her.[50] An immediate problem arose. Jan had, from an early age "wanted to be a pastor's wife," and at this point in his life, Peterson had no interest in becoming a pastor. Peterson describes Jan's desire to be a pastor's wife as about more than being married to a pastor, but an expression of a vocation in which she might meet human need and extend hospitality and God's grace. He says, "Being a pastor's wife would place her strategically at a heavily trafficked intersection between heaven and earth."[51] Peterson's description of Jan's vocational intent is intriguing. I would label his description of her work as ministry, whether ordained or not. Of course, Peterson becomes a pastor and Jan was able to pursue her vocation as a pastor's wife. Both he and Jan seem to have seen themselves as a pastoral team, working together in ministry and building the church he founded and led for many years.

What is intriguing is that he never seems to question the fact that she was most likely unpaid (though I don't know this for certain). Nor does he seem to mention whether she aspired to be a pastor herself. Given that the Petersons were married in the late 1950s, she probably never considered being a pastor since the option of ordination was very likely not open to her at the time. It may be unfair to consider this an under-told narrative for the two

---

50 Peterson, 92–97.
51 Peterson, 95.

reasons I just noted. This is, after all, Peterson's story of becoming a pastor, and both Eugene and Jan Peterson probably took it for granted that being a pastor's wife was a noble vocation and perhaps never considered the ordination of women. This memoir, however, was written in 2011. While some denominations still do not ordain women, many do. Since Peterson repeatedly mentions their work together in ministry, I found myself wondering about Jan's story. He has clearly articulated ideas about the nature and purpose of ministry, but he does not approach the issue of the ordination of women. As he looks back at his life and sees his ministry in a new light, it would be interesting to know how he views his wife's ministry.

Exercise

Can you identify any stories in your life that are under-told, because they are difficult stories, or considered unimportant, or you never questioned them because "that's how things were then"? How might a reconsideration of this under-told story revise your personal and pastoral narrative?

From Close Reading to Reinterpretation and Revision

"Reading" our life story is the first step of story care. Through a close reading of Brown Taylor's and Peterson's memoirs, we illumined the impact of confining narratives, the backstory, and under-told or untold stories on narratives of pastoral identity. The narrative of ministry that Peterson developed over time was able to sustain him, even though he faced challenges and disappointments. Brown Taylor's narrative proved unsustainable. An unsustainable practice cannot be maintained over time and leads to the depletion of natural resources.[52] We see both of these features in Brown Taylor's

---

52 OxfordDictionaries.com, s.v. "unsustainable," accessed January 8, 2018, https://en.oxforddictionaries.com/definition/unsustainable.

narrative. In the end, she could not maintain her narrative of ministry, and trying to do so depleted her resources and endangered her well-being. She felt she had no choice but to exit parish ministry.

The good news is that we can revise our stories. This is the second step in story care. This process of revision requires reinterpretation. Through a close reading of a story, we begin to see that more than one interpretation is possible. If you have practiced biblical exegesis, you have discovered the multiple meanings layered in one text that allow for varying interpretations. A close reading of our life stories likewise reveals there is more than one way to make sense of these stories than we might have noticed while in the middle of living them. This process of reinterpreting and revising life narratives has been referred to as "restorying."[53]

For some of us, the process of restorying occurs gradually over the course of our lives, though we may not be fully aware of this process.[54] In this case, we may make small edits, reinterpreting and revising our stories as we age and gain new perspectives. Life events may come to have new or revised meaning as we look back from a different vantage point. There appears to be a process of restorying at work in Peterson's memoir. He seems to have been revising his narrative as he went along. Peterson also was able to recognize and resist confining master narratives of ministry that might have resulted in an unsustainable story. By drawing on biblical concepts of church and ministry, he drew on these master narratives of what the church was or ought to be, thus giving a different backstory. Somehow, Peterson was able to revise his story as he went along so that it continued to sustain him. His memoir also reveals that he continues to engage in the process of

---

[53] Gary M. Kenyon and William L. Randall, *Restorying Our Lives: Personal Growth Through Autobiographical Reflection* (Westport, CT: Praeger, 1997), 1.
[54] Kenyon and Randall, 99–100.

restorying as he looks back over the process of becoming a pastor and finds new meanings in his life story.

For others of us, like Brown Taylor, restorying can be more dramatic, triggered by a crisis. Yet now that you know how to set about it, you need not wait for a crisis to restory your life. You can learn to engage intentionally and in an ongoing way in the process of restorying, choosing to "take authorship of your life story" and define and clarify who you are.[55] Becoming better readers of our life stories is the first step of story care. In the following chapter, we will further explore the process of revising and restorying unsustainable narratives.

Exercise

1) Imagine a publisher has just contacted you to write your pastoral memoir. You have been asked to identity the part of your story in ministry you will feature. If you can come up with a really catchy title, you will get a big bonus.

2) Take a few moments and think about the title for your memoir and whether this would cover your whole ministry, as Peterson's story does, or a portion of it, such as Brown Taylor's. Jot down your thoughts, your title, and the part of the story you are choosing to tell. Imagine chapter titles, as well as key incidents you might relate. What do your reflections reveal about your pastoral identity or your ideas of ministry?

3) Can you identify elements in your narrative, including your backstory, that are sustaining you in ministry? What strategies do you use to resisting confining narratives of ministry that might contribute to an unsustainable narrative? Are you aware of times in your life you have had to revise your story of ministry? If so, what led you to engage in this process?

---

55 Kenyon and Randall, 101.

3

Restorying
Challenging and Revising Unsustainable Narratives

Unsustainable narratives undermine our well-being. Through restorying we can challenge and revise these narratives. In this chapter I will consider two dimensions, or levels, of analysis in the restorying process: the micro and macro levels. At the micro level, our focus is on restorying our personal narratives. I consider the process of this micro-level restorying as it is represented in the last chapters of Barbara Brown Taylor's memoir, Jonathan Martin's reflections on the aftermath of his exit from ministry,[1] and my personal story.

At the macro level of restorying, we identify, challenge, and revise the master stories at work in the larger culture that contribute to unsustainable pastoral narratives. I examine the impact of two master narratives common in our culture. The first presents models and images of success in ministry, and the second frames

---

1   Jonathan Martin, *How to Survive a Shipwreck: Help Is on the Way and Love Is Already Here* (Grand Rapids: Zondervan, 2016).

the stories of clergy health and self-care. I argue that these two master narratives contribute to unsustainable pastoral narratives in ministry. To restore and sustain well-being, we must engage in both levels of the restorying process, revising personal narratives of ministry and challenging master narratives that contribute to unsustainable narratives.

Restorying Unsustainable Personal Narratives

Our life story shapes the way we view the world, and we tend not to question "why we live in terms of this story and not some other."[2] We can learn to take a more active role as authors of our own stories, rather than allowing our stories to be shaped primarily by the stories communicated to us through our families and other narrative environments in which we live our lives.[3] In order to change our lives, we must revise our life stories.[4] We will look at how the process occurs at the micro or personal level through three examples.

Keeping and Letting Go: Barbara Brown Taylor

As Brown Taylor prepared to exit parish ministry after twenty-one years, she sorted through the symbols of her ministry, as well as her convictions about it, deciding what to keep and what to let go.[5] The clerical collar, once central to her identity, was worn seldom now, saved for occasions of guest preaching. She kept her Bible, both because it remains the word of God for her and because it

---

2 Gary M. Kenyon and William L. Randall, *Restorying Our Lives: Personal Growth Through Autobiographical Reflection* (Westport, CT: Praeger, 1997), 101.
3 Kenyon and Randall, 101.
4 Kenyon and Randall, 101.
5 Brown Taylor, *Leaving Church*, 213 (see chap. 2, n. 5).

serves "as a field guide" for life and ministry.[6] Among the convictions she let go is a particular interpretation of faithfulness. Once she believed that being faithful meant living "a holier life" and calling those to whom she ministered to do the same.[7] She let go of her expectation of being an expert on "scripture and theology," and her compulsion to be at the church whenever "the doors were open, and never saying no to anyone in need."[8] She realized she had to redefine faithfulness, which had "meant ignoring my own needs and the needs of my family until they went away altogether, leaving me free to serve God without any selfish desire to drag me down."[9] She became convinced that if being faithful meant becoming someone other than herself, she couldn't do it anymore and wondered whether God might prefer her to be whole rather than good if the latter led to her complete exhaustion and self-destruction.[10]

We don't know how Taylor came to see faithfulness this way, but she tells us it was a deadly story. After twenty years in ministry, she realized that being "a professional holy person" almost killed her.[11] She came to a very important insight when she noted, "I am not sure the deadliness was in the job *as much as it was in the way I did it.*"[12] Brown Taylor finally realized that the story she carried about ministry was unsustainable. She succumbed to the temptation to see herself as entirely responsible for meeting all the spiritual needs of her parishioners and for the success of her ministry. Faithfulness in ministry was about what she did, rather than

---

6   Brown Taylor, 216.
7   Brown Taylor, 218.
8   Brown Taylor, 218–19.
9   Brown Taylor, 219.
10 Brown Taylor, 219.
11 Brown Taylor, 226.
12 Brown Taylor, 226; emphasis added.

witnessing to what God was doing. This interpretation of ministry was deadly to her. Brown Taylor came to realize that her "unwillingness to fall" was a "mistrust of the central truth of the Christian gospel: life springs from death, not only at the last, but also in the many little deaths along the way."[13]

Setting a New Course After a Shipwreck: Jonathan Martin

Pastor Jonathan Martin also discovered that his narrative of ministry was unsustainable. Unfortunately, he discovered this in the aftermath of what he calls a "shipwreck."[14] His book is more of a theological and spiritual reflection on his experience of leaving ministry than a memoir, since he gives us little detail about the exact life circumstances that occurred in this period of his life. He does tell us this: "I had failed in my marriage. I had failed my church. I had failed my friends. I sailed my own ship into the rocks—and both the relationships that mattered most to me and my calling to the church I loved were the casualties."[15]

Though we don't know much directly of Martin's narrative of ministry before his shipwreck, we get some glimpse of how he felt in the aftermath of leaving a church he had founded. No longer the one in charge, he felt incompetent.[16] No longer being the one to save the day, but feeling rather "in need of saving," he felt he "had no way out."[17] Rather than seeing himself as the savior of others, he was now in need of saving. With an oblique reference to the story of Jesus healing the man by the pool of Bethsaida

---

13 Brown Taylor, 218.
14 Martin, *How to Survive a Shipwreck*, 27.
15 Martin, 27.
16 Martin, 27.
17 Martin, 43.

(John 5), he described himself as "the lame man on the mat, in need of someone else to carry me to Jesus."[18]

Martin tells us that the years before his shipwreck had been his most successful years in ministry.[19] Following his departure from the church, he realized that though he had preached God's love to others, he had never fully known God's love in all his "broken places" and the parts of him that felt "the most unlovable."[20] Martin articulates a belief that many of us in ministry may feel but rarely confess. "My theory is that . . . the ones who spend all of our lives trying to keep the rules, have a deep suspicion that if we do feel loved and accepted, it is because we are working so hard to get it right."[21] Martin seemed to believe that the "success" of his ministry was primarily dependent on his efforts and that to "fail" at ministry was to fail God. After relinquishing his pulpit, Martin wondered, "What if God doesn't choose to save us in spite of our failings, losses, and embarrassments, but precisely through them?"[22]

Unlearning Lessons of Caregiving and Learning to Say No: My Story

After being ordained an elder, I became the pastor in charge of a small congregation. I was the always-available pastor who didn't take a day off and couldn't say no to anyone in need. At one point, I even took into the parsonage a homeless woman with two children under the age of five. Even at the time I knew it was not a good idea. After six years of being in ministry, I was burned-out, my marriage had come to an end, and I had decided to begin a

---

18 Martin, 43.
19 Martin, 84.
20 Martin, 85.
21 Martin, 85.
22 Martin, 43.

doctoral program as a way of escape. While I have no regrets about going to graduate school, my motivations were decidedly mixed. When I left the congregation that I had been serving to return to school, I felt like a failure in my personal and professional life. I had always been successful at school and I still wanted to feel successful, and being in school provided that.

I'd like to tell you that I had a great epiphany during graduate school and came to the realization that the way I took care of others was an unsustainable story. I did learn some important lessons about setting limits, attending to boundaries, and increasing my self-awareness in my clinical training in pastoral counseling, which was a required part of my doctoral program. So while I would say that I learned to make some minor revisions in my narrative of caretaking, in truth I still had great difficulty in saying no to any request made of me.

My inability to say no followed me into my academic career. By external measures, I was successful: I had published; I had been tenured; I was a popular teacher; I was seen as a good and reliable colleague and rarely refused frequent requests to take on extra projects. But several years after receiving tenure, I hit a wall. I initially chalked it up to physical exhaustion and lack of sleep as a result of the combined effect of menopause and a recently diagnosed sleep disorder. Medication to treat both of those conditions initially helped, but it was not enough. I finally had to admit I was depressed, which took some time since I had not experienced it before. I had been in counseling a number of times over the course of my life, and now returned. Through that process, I realized I was still living out a life story that was significantly shaped by difficult and traumatic events in my adolescence and early adulthood. I realized that that story could no longer sustain me and I was withering away inside. My desire to take care of and save my mother had turned into a need to care for and save the world. My sense of self-worth was dependent on it.

After a significant period in counseling and a lot of work, I was able to revise my story. Like Jonathan Martin, I have discovered that I can lose what is most dear to me and not be lost. Like Brown Taylor, I discovered that being human was enough, that I was enough. I now feel a sense of freedom and joy in my life that I am not sure I have ever felt before. I can now say no, though I still feel the need to do so very politely. I rediscovered my creative abilities and returned to writing poetry, knitting, and other creative pursuits. I enjoy my teaching more now than I have in quite a while. This process of revising my life story took several years. I suspect that was likely the case for Martin and Brown Taylor as well. Like them, I also have a much more profound sense of the depth of God's grace and love. It is no longer an idea I believe in, but a reality I experience in the depth of my being.

Reflections on Restorying Unsustainable Personal Narratives

Brown Taylor, Martin, and I all carried unsustainable narratives of ministry. Like Barbara Brown Taylor, I ignored my own needs, hoping they would simply go away. Like Jonathan Martin, I felt driven to succeed. Though I was not the pastor of a large and growing church, as Martin was, I felt the success of the church's ministry was somehow up to me. All three of us were driven by a need for control, the approval of others, and an unrecognized feeling of the need to earn God's grace through what Brown Taylor calls "exhausting goodness."[23] All three of us were forced to restory our lives and ministry.

---

23 Brown Taylor, *Leaving Church*, 219.

While I have always believed in the depth and breadth of God's love, I have not always felt the freedom to love from the depths of my soul. Like Barbara Brown Taylor, I believed that loving others meant ignoring my own needs, or at least that others' needs were more important than mine. Unfortunately, many of us believe this. For some of us, it's almost easier to think that love is transactional: that you'll love me if I love you. Connected to this is often a feeling that being good means doing good, so that our worth becomes dependent on our own efforts. Despite the fact that some of us preach and teach God's unconditional love, some of us harbor the feeling that we must earn it. What often lies underneath this feeling is shame, or a feeling that we are damaged in some way or not good enough. Many things can contribute to these feelings of shame, including trauma of various sorts, and chronic stress. But I also believe this shame is compounded by cultural narratives and scripts that say we are responsible for our own perfection. We harbor a belief that every day we *ought* to be getting better and better, and if we don't, it is a sign of our moral failure and that we are simply not enough.

Now I am convinced that God wants me to be the best human possible, not to be superhuman. My goal is to know more fully what Paul proclaims in Romans 8:38–39: that nothing can separate us from the love of God. I have not finished my journey of growing in love. It has been a struggle at times and I have felt deep pain, but through God's grace and the persistence and care of many others, I have come to a deeper sense of how God intends me to flourish. And I now feel a bit evangelistic about it! I especially feel this for many of my clergy brothers and sisters who love others deeply but still believe that this means either ignoring themselves or that a desire for flourishing in this life is a mark of selfishness.

Exercise

When have you struggled with the feeling that the success or failure of your ministry was primarily dependent on your own efforts and that to "fail at ministry" was to fail God? When have you struggled with the feeling that caring for others required you to ignore your own needs or considered these needs selfish?

Master Narratives of Success in Unsustainable Pastoral Narratives

When we examine personal narratives of ministry that are unsustainable, we may focus on the personal traits as well as the beliefs or practices of the pastor. We look at ways to change the narrative at the micro level. This is a reasonable place to begin restorying, but it is not the place to end. I believe we can find signs of a master narrative of success in ministry in all three of the narratives we have examined. The role of master narratives in developing and keeping in place unsustainable pastoral narratives is often overlooked. Common threads in all three of the narratives discussed previously include: growth as a measure of success, as well as a sense of personal responsibility for success or failure in ministry.

This master narrative of success typically emphasizes numerical and financial growth, increasing the church's attendance and budget, and the personal responsibility of the pastor to make these things happen. Author and consultant J. R. Briggs reports that many clergy experience the pressure to be successful and meet benchmarks of success established by congregational and denominational leaders.[24] According to Briggs, who leads the Epic Fail Pastors Conference, a significant number of clergy "feel

---

24 J. R. Briggs, *Fail: Finding Grace and Hope in the Midst of Ministry Failure* (Downers Grove: IL: InterVarsity Press Books, 2014), 48.

sky-high expectations and unbearable pressures and believe it impossible to meet the demands so many place on them."[25] This pervasive "culture of success" in the church is not easy to resist.[26] Briggs cites as an example "a recent issue of a well-recognized ministry magazine" that listed the "100 Largest and Fastest-Growing Churches in America," with each church "ranked by attendance" and "describing the secrets of their success and ministry growth."[27] He argues, "The three B's of current ministry success standards in North America are *buildings, bodies* and *budget*, marked by three questions: How many? How often? How much?"[28] These three questions reflect a commitment to "efficiency," a principle taken out of the world of business management.[29] Church leaders as well as laity have increasingly used such business models. The problem may not be with the model itself, but with the importance we give to it in defining our work in ministry. Briggs suggests, "The problem arises when we put an inordinate amount of emphasis on number and *thus downplay the role of stories*."[30] What he means here is that we begin to see people in terms of numbers rather than through their personal stories.

I suggest that in addition to ignoring personal stories, we also overlook the impact of the often-invisible master narratives that shape cultural values and practices. Because of the influence of the narrative environments in which we are formed and the master narrative communicated to us through these environments, we are not the sole authors of our life stories. The more immediate narrative environments of family, community, congregation, denomination,

---

25 Briggs, 48.
26 Briggs, 48.
27 Briggs, 48.
28 Briggs, 63.
29 Briggs, 63.
30 Briggs, 67.

and culture communicate master narratives that shape our understanding of ourselves and the nature of success in ministry.

Resisting Master Narratives of "Success"

Martin's, Brown Taylor's, and my own unexamined life stories and narratives of ministry all led to a departure from a congregation and an eventual redefinition of self and ministry. Only after departing from the pulpits we served were we able to begin revising our life stories, and challenging previously unexamined beliefs about ourselves and ministry. All three of us became aware of some of our dysfunctional personal narratives that led to our departures from pulpit ministry. We all made changes to our personal stories, but we only obliquely noted the influence of the larger master stories that were shaping our personal narratives. Revising personal stories may not be enough to prevent restorying unsustainable pastoral narratives if we don't also attend to the larger master narratives that influence our ideas of ministry and our measure of success.

Eugene Peterson has for many years pushed against the master narrative of success in ministry as defined by business models. In *Working the Angles,* he describes the metamorphosis of pastors into a "company of shopkeepers" who become "preoccupied with shopkeeper's concerns," such as keeping customers happy, beating the competition, and packaging "goods so the customers will lay out more money."[31] The cultural expectations of success and the idea of ministry as a profession or job are in tension with the idea of ministry as a vocation and biblical images of ministry. Living in this tension is not an easy matter, as Peterson reflects:

> How do I, as a pastor, prevent myself from thinking of my work as a job I get paid for, a job that is assigned to me by my

---

31 Eugene Peterson, *Working the Angles* (Grand Rapids: Eerdmans, 1987), 1–2.

denomination, a job that I am expected to do to the satisfaction of my congregation? . . . How do I keep the immediacy and authority of God's call in my ears when an entire culture, both secular and ecclesial, is giving me a job description? How do I keep the calling, the *vocation,* of pastor from being drowned out by job descriptions, gussied up in glossy challenges and visions and strategies, clamoring incessantly for my attention?[32]

When external measures, including the opinion of others, become the dominant measure not only of success but also of self-worth, we are in trouble. I'm not saying metrics are unimportant, but as Briggs argues, "numbers . . . cannot be the final and exclusive report card from which we derive an accurate grade of ministry."[33] The master narrative of ministry as a job or profession undergirds a personal narrative that links self-worth to success and says that failure is to be avoided at all costs.

The reality is that we do live in the tension between two competing master narratives of ministry: being successful at the job of ministry and being faithful to the call to ministry as a vocation. How do we navigate the challenges? For Peterson, meeting regularly with a group of other ministers who try to hold to biblically informed models of ministry and a sense of calling or vocation helps fight off the pressure to measure his success based primarily on numbers.

Being aware of the presence and power of master narratives of ministerial success can help us resist their influence on our personal narratives. The good news is that we do not have to wait for a crisis to begin the restorying process. To borrow some of Martin's

---

32 Peterson, *The Pastor,* 165 (see chap. 2, n. 6).
33 Briggs, *Fail,* 67, citing Michael T. Wilson and Brad Hoffman, *Prventing Minsitry Failure* (Downers Grove, IL: IVP Books, 2007), 31.

metaphorical language, we may be able to start the restorying process when we begin to notice a storm brewing, rather than waiting until we are adrift in the ocean, clinging to wreckage. I want to encourage you to read your own personal stories more deeply in the midst of your ministry so that you can make revisions to them before a crisis forces you into a restorying process.

Some master narratives, such as cultural measures of success, when reinforced by some certain dimensions of our personal stories can potentially have a negative impact not only on our life stories but also on our health and well-being.

Exercise

Can you begin to identify some of the master narratives that influence your view of what it means to be successful in ministry? How is success in ministry measured—by you and by others? Where do these measures come from? What values do they reflect? And what theology of the church undergirds them?

Master Narratives of Clergy Health and Wellness

A second interconnected set of master narratives that contribute to unsustainable practices are those that deal with clergy bodies, health, and wellness. These master narratives are less evident in the memoirs we examined, though there are some oblique references to the physical and mental toll of ministry in both Brown Taylor's and Martin's stories. We don't just tell our stories of ministry; we live them in our bodies. We are *embodied* stories. We live out our stories in and through our bodies, and how we think about our bodies affects their health.

Most of us are aware that the Christian church has not always done such a good job of paying attention to the body. We have sometimes spiritualized the body or split body and soul. We notice this in the ambivalence about clergy bodies in general and how we think about our own clergy bodies. For example, while wearing liturgical garments is a historical practice, I have often heard women clergy say they wear robes to avoid comments about their clothing or bodies or so as not to be a distraction in worship. At times, I think we like to pretend that clergy don't have bodies. After all, clergy are supposed to be spiritual leaders, and does spirituality have anything to do with bodies? (Of course it does! But we pretend one can manage without a body and that our spiritual side is distinct from the body and superior to it.)

Yet in addition to the troublesome stories about bodies in the Christian tradition, we also have a counter story that honors the body. Both incarnation and resurrection remind us of the importance of bodies to God and God's work of salvation. Our faith affirms "that everybody is worthy of blessing and care and [that] through the needs of the body, we are invited into relationship with God.[34] How might we draw more deeply on these dimensions of the Christian tradition and construct an alternate story of caring for and loving bodies, including our own?

An added difficulty is that Christian stories about the body are not the only ones that influence us. We gather stories about bodies through the narrative environments of our families, the subcultures of which we are a part, and the larger American culture. We are surrounded by media images of impossible bodies: men with washboard abs on the cover of fitness magazines; female models, already thin, Photoshopped to impossible and inhuman proportions. Very rarely do we see pictures in magazines of old bodies, infirm bodies, or differently abled bodies.

---

34 Stephanie Paulsell, *Honoring the Body: Meditations on Christian Practice* (San Francisco: Jossey-Bass, 2002), xiv, 10.

Paying attention to clergy bodies and the stories we tell about them is critical because many clergy bodies are in trouble. While we must pay attention to clergy health and the lack of it, I am concerned about the way we tell the story of clergy health. Undergirding the story of clergy health are two master narratives that play a large role in our culture. The first of these that I consider influential is the medical model of health. The second master narrative that has arisen in the past few decades is a particular view of wellness called the "wellness syndrome."[35] These two influential master narratives are connected to each other. We will look at how these master narratives may contribute to unsustainable pastoral narratives.

A Story of Clergy Health: The Medical Model

The medical model can be defined in various ways, but is usually understood as employing scientific methods in order to observe, describe, recognize, and treat symptoms, as well as identify the source of an illness and its treatment.[36] The medical model itself is not necessarily the problem. Advances in medicine have vastly improved lives in the United States and around the world, so I am not advocating entirely abandoning a medical model. How we interpret this model, however, can become problematic; and a certain version of it, in which treating illness is primarily about the removal of symptoms, can begin to function as a master narrative and constrain the way we tell our own story of illness and health.

---

35 Carl Cedarström and André Spicer, *The Wellness Syndrome* (Cambridge, UK: Polity Press, 2015), 6.

36 Premal Shah and Deborah Mountain, "The Medical Model Is Dead—Long Live the Medical Model," *British Journal of Psychiatry* 191, no. 5 (October 2007): 375–77; https://doi.org/10.1192/bjp.bp.107.037242.

CHAPTER 3

The story of clergy health has largely been communicated through the medical model. Reports on clergy health generally report on the medical conditions affecting clergy health. As a result, we end up with a picture of clergy ill-health. Research on clergy health since the 1980s shows a marked decline in clergy health in contrast to earlier studies in the 1950s.[37] Clergy report higher rates of the following conditions than the general population: obesity, high blood pressure, high cholesterol, stress, and depression.[38] The story of clergy health is largely told through the frame of the medical model. The medical model of health serves as a master narrative for the way we discuss health in general in the United States. While there are advantages to a medical model of health, it has limitations when it is the primary way we tell the story of clergy health.

Let's look at an example of how the story of clergy health is told through the lens of the medical model. One article presents a picture of clergy health, or the lack of it, in the form of a medical case study.

> The patient: 51-year-old male with symptoms of depression, the patient has high blood pressure and is overweight, presenting a heightened risk of heart disease and other illnesses. He works 60–70 hours a week in a sedentary job, does not currently engage in any physical exercise, and reports considerable work-related stress. Patient is married, with three children, one of whom expresses interest in following

---

[37] Bob Wells, "Which Way to Clergy Health?" Sustaining Pastoral Excellence, accessed June 22, 2016, https://www.faithandleadership.com/programs/spe/resources/dukediv-clergyhealth.html?printable=true.
[38] The June 2015 Clergy Health Survey conducted by the Center for Health of the United Methodist General Board of Pension and Health Benefits.

patient's career path. Patient expresses little enthusiasm for encouraging child to do so.[39]

The article, written in 2002, goes on to note that this profile is not of an individual, "but a statistically based overview of the typical Lutheran pastor,"[40] and a similar picture of poor health is found among clergy of most Christian denominations in the United States.[41]

The story of clergy health told here focuses primarily on symptoms of *ill*-health. The key findings of the June 2017 Clergy Health Survey show that the percentage of clergy dealing with obesity, high blood pressure, high cholesterol, stress, and depression has not declined significantly over the last five years.[42] Each of these symptoms may point to the presence of one or more underlying conditions or illnesses. We also now know that many of these symptoms occur as a result of high levels of stress.[43] I find it interesting that a report on clergy health primarily presents a list of symptoms of ill health. An implicit assumption of the medical model is that health is the absence of disease and restoration of health is the reduction or removal of symptoms. This seems a rather limited view of health. Instead of considering overall well-being and happiness, we are only concerned with the ways we are not sick; but absence of sickness does not mean we are healthy, and it certainly does not mean we are flourishing. It's an important distinction.

---

39 Wells, "Which Way to Clergy Health?"
40 Wells.
41 Wells.
42 "Well-Being Survey of the Methodist Church Active U.S. Clergy—2017," Wespath, Center for Health, https://www.wespath.org/assets/1/7/5058.pdf.
43 Wells, "Which Way to Clergy Health?"

My point in sketching this story of the medical model of clergy health is not to debunk it, or to tell you to forget about your doctor. I do want to suggest that the medical model of clergy health tends to focus on problems, on what is missing, or on simply listing symptoms. Another dimension of the medical model is a tendency to focus on the individual patient. It often does not take into account social or environmental factors that may contribute to ill-health. The problem is that we can't do without the medical model: we do need to diagnose and treat symptoms of ill-health.

Denominational leaders and researchers have been rightly concerned about the impact of poor clergy health on individuals and congregations. How can you expect a thriving congregation when the person leading it is overworked and unfulfilled? Since the problem of clergy health has been identified, a good number of books on the topic have been published, and many are excellent. Some of them include a discussion of spiritual practices, yet still reinforce the medical model, as in the earlier example.[44] A number of denominations have developed programs to improve clergy health, and some of these efforts have been moderately successful. The 2017 United Methodist report on clergy health does contain some good news, including increased levels of physical activity among clergy.[45] These good results are primarily attributed to the variety of wellness prorams offered through the Center for Health, as well as health initiatives offered by individual United Methodist Annual Conferences.[46]

---

44 See, for example, *The Right Road: Life Choices for Clergy,* written by Dr. Gwen Wagstrom Halaas, a physician and director of ministerial health and wellness for the Evangelical Church in America (Minneapolis: Augsburg Fortress Press, 2004).
45 "Well-Being Survey of the Methodist Church Active U.S. Clergy, 2017."
46 See www.wespath.org/center-for-health/ for programs available in the United Methodist Church.

Typically, these programs focus on behavioral changes, including changing one's diet, increasing exercise, and reducing stress. And they have shown some success. However, overall clergy health has not shown significant improvement.[47] Researchers in the Duke clergy study report that "clergy recognize the importance of caring for themselves, but doing so takes a back seat to fulfilling their vocational responsibilities."[48] Many pastors feel they need permission to take the time to attend to their health and "equate self-care with selfishness."[49] It is clear that lack of knowledge is not the problem. By now, most of us know the basic advice for improving our health: eat right, exercise, reduce stress. The quotation from the Duke study reinforces what we saw in the life stories of clergy we have examined through memoir and my own recollections. Knowing what to do is not enough when we are surrounded by powerful stories about ministry that require us to be successful, good, or self-sacrificial.

A Story of Wellness and the Wellness Syndrome

Many denominations now encourage clergy to take care of their health and may inquire about plans for self-care as a part of clergy evaluation or ordination processes. I applaud these developments, and perhaps had some of these been in place when I was ordained, the bishop praising the Conference secretary might have done so without referring so glowingly to the ridiculous and inhuman number of hours he worked. However, I am bothered by something we don't talk about much. What happens when I don't manage to eat right, exercise regularly, stave off excess stress, be immune to

---

47 Duke Clergy Health Study 2014.
48 *Duke Today* staff, "Clergy Health: Who Cares for the Caregivers?" *Duke Today*, June 28, 2012, http://today.duke.edu/2012/06/clergyhealth.
49 *Duke Today*, "Clergy Health."

the occasional depression, or pray as often as I ought? Who is to blame? The easy answer is: myself. Yet I have seen how this answer can lead to a limiting, problematic story. For example, I have seen gifted seminary students who are deeply committed to the church quail with fear about going before United Methodist Conference Boards of Ordained Ministry. Their fear stems not from worry that their answers to theological questions will be inadequate, but rather, their worry is linked to a BMI (body mass index) number higher than it should be. Not measuring up to an expected health standard can be experienced as a personal failing and, more specifically, as a moral failing.

Health has become a moral issue. To some extent, behaviors that impact health, such as addiction, have long been seen as a moral issue. In this case, the medical model has been helpful in describing addiction as a disease with a set of symptoms, risk factors, and prescribed treatments. What is different now, according to Cedarström and Spicer, is that achieving and maintaining wellness has now "become a moral demand—about which we are constantly and tirelessly reminded."[50] Their concern is not with wellness itself, but rather the ideology that has formed around wellness. They argue that this "ideological element of wellness is particularly visible when considering the prevailing attitudes towards those who fail to look after their bodies" as "lazy, feeble, or weak willed."[51]

Wellness has become "a moral imperative," an obligation rather than something we choose in order to tend the marvelous gift of our bodies.[52] Once wellness becomes a personal moral obligation, it gives rise to the "wellness command," which feels as

---

50 Cedarström and Spicer, *The Wellness Syndrome*, 3.
51 Cedarström and Spicer, 3.
52 Cedarström and Spicer, 4, 5.

if it is imposed from the outside rather than arising as an internal motivation.[53] This wellness command now begins to work against us and can give rise to what Cedarström and Spicer call "the wellness syndrome."[54] Building on the definition of a syndrome as "a group of symptoms that work together," the "wellness syndrome" describes a set of symptoms, including "anxiety, self-blame, and guilt," that arise in response to the wellness command.[55] The wellness syndrome reflects a view of the individual as "autonomous, potent, strong-willed and relentlessly striving to improve."[56] Such a view of the individual is part of a larger cultural master story that sees human beings as autonomous individuals responsible for their own self-development and well-being.

An emphasis on personal responsibility is also undergirded by the values and mind-set of a free market economy in which success is tied to individual achievement and beating out the competition.[57] Healthier workers are more productive workers. Many companies now encourage their "employees to get into a state of peak employment."[58] According to a 2013 RAND study on workplace wellness, more than half of US companies with more than fifty staff members offer some kind of wellness program to their employees, while "another survey found that 70 percent of Fortune 200 Companies provide employee fitness programs."[59] Companies in the United States spend billions of dollars on

---

53 Cedarström and Spicer, 6.
54 Cedarström and Spicer, 6.
55 Cedarström and Spicer, 6.
56 Cedarström and Spicer, 6.
57 Cedarström and Spicer, 6.
58 Cedarström and Spicer, 35.
59 Soren Matteke et al., *Workplace Wellness Programs Study: Final Report* (Santa Monica: RAND, 2013), cited in Cedarström and Spicer, *The Wellness Syndrome*, 35.

programs that include "diet groups, diet counseling, cafeterias with health food, exercise breaks at work, on-site gym facilities and smoking cessation" programs.[60] Some US denominations have now developed similar programs to encourage clergy wellness.[61] The United Methodists use a program called Healthflex to encourage wellness. The ELCA uses Portico benefits. These are just two of the fifty-six programs for clergy health in Protestant denominations in the United States.[62]

On the surface, such an emphasis on wellness in the workplace seems like a good idea, and the availability of health promotion programs may be an additional benefit for employees. However, the benefits of wellness programs to employers is not entirely clear.[63] Such programs do impact the image of the ideal worker: the productive employee is the fit employee.[64] Those who are less fit and may be overweight are "automatically seen as inactive and unproductive."[65] The goal of perfect fitness is rarely achieved, and the constant pursuit of it may produce anxiety and self-reproach for never achieving one's goal.[66] Once wellness becomes a command, we are quickly ensnared in the "wellness syndrome," in which our lack of wellness becomes a personal moral failure, leading to self-blame and anxiety.[67]

---

60 Cedarström and Spicer, *The Wellness Syndrome*, 35, citing World Economic Forum, *Working Toward Wellness* (2007), http://www.healthaction.net/wellness/workingtowardwellness-business-rationale.pdf, 20–21.
61 The UMC, the ELCA, and others.
62 Matthew J. Edlund, "What We Talk About When We Talk About Health," *Psychology Today*, July 11, 2015, https://www.psychologytoday.com/blog/the-power-rest/201507/what-we-talk-about-when-we-talk-about-health.
63 Cedarström and Spicer, *The Wellness Syndrome*, 37.
64 Cedarström and Spicer, 37.
65 Cedarström and Spicer, 38.
66 Cedarström and Spicer, 39.
67 Cedarström and Spicer, 6.

This notion of the wellness syndrome well describes the anxiety I see in ministry students and candidates for ordination regarding their self-care, which is almost primarily focused on the body. I do believe we want to encourage clergy and all human beings to be good stewards of the gift of health, which includes attending to physical health, as well as emotional and spiritual health. My concern is that even the church can get caught up in the wellness syndrome. Embedded in this view of wellness is an anthropological assumption, or a view of human beings that holds individuals personally responsible for their well-being, and assumes self-improvement primarily occurs through our own efforts. Such a view also ignores the systemic problems that make good health so much harder for some people to enjoy than others. The problem with such a view is that it contradicts a Christian perspective in which health and well-being are gifts of grace and not a result of innate human capacities or effort.

Exercise

If you have been encouraged by your congregation or denomination to develop a self-care plan that includes improving your physical heath, in what ways have you found or not found this supportive and helpful? What are some of the messages you receive from the larger culture that communicate you are personally responsible for your health, good or ill?

Challenging the Power of Master Narratives

Restorying our lives involves not only a closer reading of our personal narrative, but also identifying and challenging the influence of the master narratives about success in ministry or clergy health that influence our personal stories while operating largely outside of our awareness.

Only by examining the master narratives that impact us, often without our awareness, can we decide which of these stories we will keep and which we will reject. We can begin to uncover the influence of master narratives on our personal narratives by asking ourselves some of the following questions:[68]

- Where did I learn this way of thinking, believing, and behaving/acting?
- What authority figures or authoritative teaching reinforced these beliefs and behaviors?
- Who modeled this behavior for me?
- How was I rewarded for acting in accordance with these beliefs?
- Was I disciplined in some way for behaving in ways contrary to these beliefs?
- Have I ever questioned these beliefs?
- Who and what contributed to and reinforced a particular story I hold about myself?

Many of us have experienced the power of the cultural narrative that shapes our ideas of success in ministry and notions of clergy health and self-care, even if we are unable to name that narrative. The master narratives of success and clergy wellness can become intertwined, so that the successful clergy person—with the bigger, better church—is also expected to be the picture of health. In this narrative, self-care becomes a moral obligation, and good health, or wellness, the assumed reward and ultimate good. The intertwining of these narratives conflates success, health, and well-being. What these narratives also have in common is an

---

[68] Some of these questions are adapted from Scheib, *Pastoral Care*, 91.

assumption that this state of well-being is a personal achievement that comes about as a result of the intentional development of our innate capacities through hard work and personal effort. This narrative of well-being, which is very influential in our culture, has deep and ancient roots. A Christian theological understanding of well-being provides a different story, and we turn to this narrative in the next chapter.

4

A Christian Vision of Flourishing

Once we have recognized how the personal and cultural stories (such as the one about health and wellness) contribute to unsustainable narratives in our lives, what then? One strategy is to push back against powerful cultural stories to maintain the integrity of our own stories. We can also connect our story to a theological vision of a well-lived, flourishing life. Yet, as we have seen through the memoirs we examined, we may be living out a version of the Christian story that is still under the strong influence of master narratives contrary to flourishing. Both Barbara Brown Taylor and Jonathan Martin were not only Christians but ordained ministers, as many of you reading this probably are. And while both of them (and perhaps you) were deeply committed to the powerful Christian story, they both found themselves getting lost in an interpretation of that story that made them feel overwhelmingly responsible for the well-being of others. The consequences of that story felt like failure. What helped them find a way up and out of the hold of these stories was letting go of a particular way of seeing themselves and God and being open to new understandings of both.

CHAPTER 4

Jonathan Martin realized that he had to let go of his life as he had known it, to "go all the way under—into the depths of God," his own soul, and "into the depths of life itself."[1] Once he let go of clinging to the wreckage of his life, he discovered: "It is possible to fail, and not have our faith fail us. It is possible to lose our lives, and not lose our souls."[2] Brown Taylor came to a similar awareness after failing to live up to her own expectation. She discovered that being human is enough, and it was redemptive. "When we are able to trust the gospel that our human love of God and one another is the sum total of what we are put on earth to do, and that we have everything we need to be human, then redeeming things will continue to happen, both because and in spite of us."[3]

Both Martin and Brown Taylor came to realize that at least some of their suffering is self-inflicted and that what God wants for them is to flourish in the depths of God's love. Both of them revised not only their personal stories but also their stories about God. Not only did they free themselves from the hold of master narratives that confine their stories; they also freed God from being required to bless these stories. My experience is similar to these authors'. Not only have I experienced the freedom to be a more authentic self as God intends; I have also freed God to be God, rather than conforming God to my ideas of God. This has led me to a deeper experience of my own well-being and a revised Christian vision of flourishing, which we explore in this chapter.

---

1 Jonathan Martin, *How to Survive a Shipwreck: Help Is On the Way and Love Is Already Here* (Grand Rapids: Zondervan, 2016), 23.
2 Martin, 32.
3 Brown Taylor, *Leaving Church*, 220 (see chap. 2, n. 5).

Visions of Flourishing

What does a Christian vison of flourishing look like? Throughout the history of the church, visions of flourishing can be traced through the doctrines of eschatology and salvation. Eschatology deals with the end of history and the fulfillment of God's promise of flourishing. Salvation is the restoration of the divine image with us damaged by the fall, which makes our reconciliation with God possible. An ongoing debate in Christian theology is the extent to which we experience God's promise of flourishing in this life versus the next.

Two Views of Christian Flourishing: Now or Later

The Christian tradition reflects different understandings of eschatology and salvation. The kingdom of God is the image or metaphor most often used to describe God's eschatological intent for the restoration and well-being of creation. Some biblical texts envision the kingdom as a future promise, others as already breaking into this world. An abiding tension in eschatology is whether the kingdom is a present reality, a future promise, or both. We can find biblical references to both views.

More theological attention has been paid to the idea that God's promises will not be fulfilled until some future time.[4] On the personal level, this means we experience our heavenly reward after death, rather than in this life. On a cosmic level, the transformation of the world comes at the end of time, when God's kingdom

---

4   Jürgen Moltmann, "Eschatology and Pastoral Care," in Rodney J. Hunter, gen. ed., *The Dictionary of Pastoral Care and Counseling* (Nashville: Abingdon Press, 1990), 360. See also Ellen T. Charry, *God and the Art of Happiness* (Grand Rapids: Eerdmans, 2010), ix.

CHAPTER 4

comes on earth.[5] An other-worldly view of God's flourishing is only one strand in the Christian tradition.

In addition to the doctrine of eschatology, the language of salvation is also used to describe the present dimension of God's promise of flourishing. For some of us, the language of salvation is meaningful and effectively communicates God's promise of well-being in this life as well as the next. For others, the idea of salvation is linked to avoiding hell and damnation and being delivered to a beatific life after death. Such a vision has little focus on happiness in this life.

Many theologians in the Western Christian tradition have been a bit nervous about claiming God's promise of well-being in this life, and have paid far less attention to it than to attaining eternal happiness.[6] We can readily find expressions of this view of well-being as a promise for the next life in hymns. One example is an American classic, "Poor Wayfaring Stranger," in which the wayfarer travels through a "world of woe," but experiences reunion with loved ones and bliss in the next life. Another example is found in the well-known hymn "For All the Saints," which depicts the victorious faithful coming to rest in paradise.[7]

I highlight a reading of the Christian story in which flourishing is a gift we can experience in this life, and is not reserved only for life after death. God's promise of flourishing is deeply embedded in the biblical witness and runs throughout Christian theological tradition from Augustine to the present. English mystic Julian of Norwich (1342–1416) came to a deep conviction of God's promise of flourishing in the midst of suffering. While she was deathly

---

5 Charry, *God and the Art of Happiness*, ix.
6 Charry, ix.
7 Wikipedia, s.v. "For All the Saints," accessed January 8, 2018, https://en.wikipedia.org/wiki/For_All_the_Saints.

ill, she received a vision of well-being, which she expressed in the words "All shall be well, and all shall be well, and all manner of things shall be well."[8] Her vision has persisted throughout the centuries, echoing the human desire for a world in which all will flourish.[9] Julian's vision of well-being is informed by a deeply held faith in the abundance of God's love for each of us and for all of creation.

We need thoughtful, sustained reflection on Christian concepts of well-being in this life to address the imbalanced focus on eschatological happiness as a future promise.[10] Theologian Ellen Charry, who has contributed to such reflection, is deeply committed to retrieving concepts of temporal well-being, not simply as theoretical concepts, but in ways that transform our daily living.[11] Charry's commitment to a revised Christian vision of "happiness" is not only scholarly, but arises from her own experience following the death of her husband of forty years.[12] In the midst of suffering and grief, she wondered whether she and others like her "can ever be happy again in this life, or whether life amounts to no more than a vale of tears simply to be slogged through somehow in hopes of a heavenly reward."[13] I, too, have struggled with this question. Are we all just "poor wayfaring strangers" or can we experience God's promises of comfort, peace, and happiness in this world? When Charry uses the word *happiness*, the term does not simply mean a positive mood or transitory pleasures, but a way of being in the

---

8 Julian of Norwich, *Showings,* trans. Edmund Colledge and James Walsh, Classics of Western Spirituality (Mahwah, NJ: Paulist Press, 1978), 225.
9 Julian of Norwich, 225.
10 I share this conviction with Ellen Charry. See Charry, *God and the Art of Happiness.*
11 Charry.
12 Charry.
13 Charry.

world rooted in God.[14] Happiness and flourishing as dimensions of salvation are solidly biblical concepts, but the focus on Christian salvation as otherworldly happiness and heavenly reward has left a gap.

Exercise

Identify a couple of hymns that convey a sense of promise or well-being in the next life. Now try finding some that highlight an experience of God's promise in this life.

A Competing Vision of Happiness: The Self-Realization Model

A Christian vision of flourishing is not the only one to which we are exposed, as we saw in the previous chapters. Various narratives of flourishing, including those couched in the language of success and health, abound in our culture and fill the gap left by a lack of theological reflection on happiness in this life. One of the influential versions of a narrative of well-being holds that the capacity to flourish is innate and that well-being is a result of our own effort. I refer to this version of the self-realization model to distinguish it from the theological vision of flourishing presented here. Expression of this self-realization model can be found in ancient Greek philosophy and contemporary positive psychology. Both philosophical and psychological versions of this vision of well-being have been influential from ancient times to our own.

The self-realization model sees humans as basically good and having an innate capacity for growth that can be fully realized through intentional development. This theological anthropology is rooted in ancient Greek philosophy and religion, which understand humans as having a capacity for self-awareness, insight, and growth

---

14 Charry.

through their own resources.[15] I am reminded of a phrase I associate with humanistic psychology as I knew it in the 1970s: "Every day in every way, I am getting better and better."[16] It originated with Emile Coue, a psychologist from the turn of the nineteenth century. The belief in the possibility of our self-improvement is longstanding and persistent. A consequence of this view is that we are held responsible for our own flourishing or lack of it. I seek a theological alternative to a self-realization vision of happiness that sees happiness as a human achievement, well-being as a moral imperative, and failure to be happy or healthy as a moral failing.

Exercise

What examples of this self-realization model of flourishing come to mind for you? Examples can often be found in the self-help section of bookstores. How have you felt influenced by this view? Was this a positive or negative experience?

Reclaiming a Theological Vision of Flourishing in This Life

To flourish is "to grow luxuriantly" and "to thrive."[17] In a Christian vision of flourishing, divine love—rather than, say, concerted human effort—is the ground of the flourishing and well-being of all

---

15 Bjorn Rabjerg, "Evil Understood as the Absence of Freedom: Outlines of a Lutheran Anthropology and Ontology" in Eve-Marie Becker, Jan Dietrich, and Bo Kristian Holm, eds., *What Is Human? Theological Encounters with Anthropology* (Göttingen: Vandenhoeck & Ruprecht, 2017), 196–97.

16 Emile Coue. See Julian Rosser, "Everyday In Every Way I'm Getting Better and Better," *Present Outlook* (blog), accessed January 8, 2018, http://presentoutlook.com/day-by-day-in-every-way-im-getting-better-and-better/.

17 Merriam-Webster.com, s.v. "flouris," accessed January 8, 2018, https://www.merriam-webster.com/dictionary/flourish.

creation. I define flourishing as: *dwelling and growing in love of God, self, and other.* Flourishing is a process, not a fixed state. Through divine grace God makes possible moral, spiritual, and psychological healing for individuals, families, and communities and enhances the well-being of the whole society.[18] God desires our flourishing. Flourishing is meant to be a joyous experience, not a hard grind. God's joy overflows into our lives.[19] When we are flourishing, we see ourselves through God's eyes as beloved. We are free to be fully human, as God intends, not more or less. Flourishing frees us to love and be loved. All this is a gift of grace.

My understanding of the character of divine love draws on the work of theologian Thomas Jay Oord. Love is intentional action in response to God's love for us, and its goal is well-being.[20] The purpose of love is to promote well-being or flourishing.[21] Our loving actions are in response to God's prior acts of love. We can love because God first loved us. By characterizing the response of love as "sympathetic/empathetic," Oord is defining love as "inherently relational."[22] Love is not a moral obligation: we are not required to love in order to receive love. The love that makes flourishing

---

[18] While I am drawing on Charry's definition here, I have modified it significantly. For her definition of Christian happiness, or what she calls "asherism," see Charry, *God and the Art of Happiness*, xi.

[19] Terence E. Fretheim, "God, Creation, and the Pursuit of Happiness" in Brent A. Strawn, ed. *The Bible and the Pursuit of Happiness* (New York: Oxford University Press, 2012), 54.

[20] Oord's definition: "To love is to act intentionally in sympathetic/empathetic response to God and others to promote over all wellbeing." Thomas Jay Oord, *The Nature of Love: A Theology* (St. Louis: Chalice Press, 2010), 17.

[21] See also Karen D. Scheib, *Pastoral Care: Telling the Stories of Our Lives* (Nashville: Abingdon Press, 2016), 53–55, for a fuller discussion of Oord's definition of love.

[22] Oord, *The Nature of Love*, 21.

possible is not transactional (I'll love you if you love me). Our love freely given is as an ethical response to the divine love we have received.

What Christians have thought and written about flourishing is a long and complex conversation. In what follows, I review select resources within the Christian tradition that contribute to my theological vision of flourishing. You might think the Bible is a good place to begin to discover a Christian vision of flourishing, but it is only recently that scholars have paid much attention to biblical notions of flourishing. Since most of the recent biblical scholarship on the topic uses the term *happiness* to denote what I mean by flourishing, the word *happiness* will appear frequently in the following discussion.[23] Because I see flourishing as made possible by divine love, we explore the work of select theologians who connect the concepts of love and flourishing following a review of some biblical sources. I look at the contributions of Augustine of Hippo, Martin Luther, and John Wesley, as well as draw on contemporary theologians, such as Charry and Oord.

A Brief Note on Language

The English words *well-being*, *flourishing*, and *happiness*, which are often used interchangeably, are all imprecise translations of Hebrew and Greek terms that often have more complex meanings than the contemporary meanings of the corresponding English words. I'd even say they have misled us into thinking that happiness, flourishing, and well-being are something different from what the Bible actually teaches. And so we have false expectations.

"Happy are those whose hope is the God of Jacob," the psalmist declares (Ps 146:5). The Hebrew word often translated as "happy" or "blessed" is *asher*, which can also refer to flourishing

---

23 See, for example, Strawn, *The Bible and the Pursuit of Happiness*.

or well-being found in relationship with God.[24] The Greek word *makarios*, which appears repeatedly in the Beatitudes found in the Gospels of Matthew and Luke, has traditionally been translated as "blessed," but is increasingly rendered as "happy."[25] In addition to these terms, there are many others that might contribute to a discussion of happiness.[26]

One of the Greek terms that is translated as flourishing, well-being, or happiness is *eudaimonia*.[27] What Aristotle meant by happiness had to do with virtue and a life well lived. It described an enduring state of well-being.[28] Another Greek term also used to describe "the happy or blessed life" is *hēdonē*, usually defined as a transitory state of pleasure dependent on the presence of external things, like wealth.[29] Aristotle characterized the good or flourishing life as an "eudaimonic life," meaning a virtuous life rather than an "enjoyable life filled with enjoyable sensations."[30] In Greek philosophy, these two terms sometimes even represented opposite or contradictory views of a happy or well-lived life. Biblical thinking about happiness is not restricted to concepts of *eudaimonia* or *hēdonē*, though these concepts have sometimes been applied to discussion of well-being, flourishing, or happiness in the Bible.

---

24 Charry, *God and the Art of Happiness*, xi.
25 Carl R. Holladay, "The Beatitudes: Happiness and the Kingdom of God," in Strawn, *The Bible and the Pursuit of Happiness*, 144.
26 See, for example, "Appendix: A Biblical Lexicon of Happiness" in Strawn, *The Bible and the Pursuit of Happiness*, 323–70.
27 Strawn, "Introduction: The Bible and . . . Happiness?" in *The Bible and the Pursuit of Happiness*, 13.
28 Strawn, "Introduction," 15.
29 Strawn, 13.
30 Strawn, 13.

The Bible on Happiness: A Few Thoughts

When you think of biblical stories, especially those in the Old Testament, are happy endings the first thing that comes to mind? While the biblical story starts out well, with beautiful images of a diverse, vibrant creation full of all kinds of creatures and human beings strolling amid this beauty with God, the story quickly turns sour. Within the first few chapters of Genesis, we have disobedience to God, expulsion from paradise, betrayal, and murder. Given this beginning, one might well wonder what, if anything, the Bible says about happiness. Is happiness a characteristic of God? Does God want happiness and flourishing for us, and if so, what does this look like? It turns out the Bible has many things to say about happiness, well-being, and flourishing, more than I can consider here, so I will mention only a few.[31] As you might imagine, the perspectives of the Old and New Testaments are somewhat different.

Joy in Creation

In the beginning is God, who calls creation into being. According to biblical scholar Terence Fretheim, God takes joy in creation.[32] He declares, "God is happy—or pleased, delighted, or joyful."[33] While Fretheim pays particular attention to the creation accounts, he also cites numerous other texts and situations in which God delights, rejoices, or takes pleasure in his people and creation, showing that happiness or joy is more broadly "characteristic of divine life."[34] Perhaps we don't often think of God as

---

31 For a fuller treatment of happiness in the Bible, see Strawn, *The Bible and the Pursuit of Happiness*.
32 Terence E. Fretheim, "God, Creation, and the Pursuit of Happiness" in Strawn, *The Bible and the Pursuit of Happiness*, 38.
33 Fretheim, 33.
34 Fretheim, 34–35.

joyful or as being affected by what happens in the world. Fretheim points to numerous Old Testament texts "where God is genuinely affected by what happens in God's world" (Gen 6:6-7; Mic 7:18; Isa 42:14).[35] What difference might it make if we imaged God as joyful or happy? Fretheim wonders if "an increased emphasis on divine joy" might have a positive effect on "the preaching and teaching of the church and the well-being of Christians."[36] Might such an emphasis provide a more complex image of God than one that focuses primarily on God's unhappiness at human sin?[37]

God's happiness and enjoyment of creation is extended to creation so that "pleasure and playfulness are built into the structure of things."[38] God wants happiness and well-being for us, who are created in the divine image.[39] The happiness God gifts human beings through creation has a relational dimension, and the vision of human well-being conveyed in the stories of creation in Genesis "focuses on well-functioning relationships at all levels of existence."[40] While some biblical texts indicate that happiness or joy can be threatened or lost, other texts suggest that "happiness can include healing" and that "new dimensions of joy," such as forgiveness, comfort, or salvation, are brought into being by God's action.[41]

A Prophetic Vision of Happiness: Isaiah

Isaiah's vision of happiness confirms the conviction that "happiness is grounded in God" and "humanity shares in and imitates the

---

35 Fretheim, 36.
36 Fretheim, 37.
37 Fretheim, 37.
38 Fretheim, 55.
39 Fretheim, 45, 55.
40 Fretheim, 46.
41 Fretheim, 49.

divine joy."[42] Four elements comprise Isaiah's vision of happiness: an "intimate, harmonious relationship with God; a secure, prosperous, and joyous home life; . . . a peaceful and just community in which to live; and hope for the future."[43] While we must recall that the context in which Isaiah's vision of happiness is articulated is in the midst of "the very difficult conditions existing in the postexilic community," his vision of happiness or flourishing is not simply an eschatological vision, but a promise for this life as well.[44]

In Isaiah's vision in Isaiah 65:17–25, which begins with a vision of "new heavens and a new earth" (v. 17a), God's joy in creation is to be repeated in a new creation and the deliverance of God's people.[45] Again we see a relational view of happiness in which God's happiness is interconnected with human happiness.[46] Human happiness is grounded in relationship with God.[47] This relationship between God and God's people is conceived of as a nearly wordless relationship (Isa 65:2–4), but is also sustained through worship (Isa 30:29; 56:7), as well as obedience to Torah.[48]

The relational dimension of happiness is not limited to God and God's people but also extends to the family and community. A happy home is a secure home, and one in which a family gathers together around good food and drink is a second feature of Isaiah's vision of happiness.[49] The happiness of the home is also extended to the broader community, which experiences happiness through

---

42 Jacqueline Lapsley, "A Happy Blend: Isaiah's Vision of Happiness (and Beyond)" in Strawn, *The Bible and the Pursuit of Happiness*, 77–78.
43 Lapsley, 79.
44 Lapsley, 79.
45 Lapsley, 80.
46 Lapsley, 80.
47 Lapsley, 83.
48 Lapsley, 82–83.
49 Lapsley, 83.

justice, peace, and abundance.[50] Hope for the future, the fourth feature of Isaiah's vision of happiness, is promised through the gift of children and being remembered, both by one's children and the community as a whole.[51]

Biblical scholar Jacqueline Lapsley highlights two additional features of Isaiah's vision of happiness relevant to the vision of flourishing I propose. First, there is no room in Isaiah's vision for "the quasi-nihilism that undergirds so much of our culture," namely, that happiness is either a product to be sold or an illusion.[52] Second, she points out that Isaiah's vision of happiness, and that of the Old Testament, "is not predicated on orientation of the other at the expense of the self," in contrast to some "versions of Christian ethics that overemphasize the emptying of the self."[53] Lapsley asserts that in Isaiah's vision, and in the overall "*biblical* vision, true happiness for the individual is not really possible apart from a happy communal life."[54]

The Beatitudes: "Happy Are . . ."

The Beatitudes, which appear in different versions in both Matthew's and Luke's Gospels, have played a central role in shaping Christian perspectives of flourishing or happiness.[55] The sayings that comprise the Beatitudes are found in a slightly different version in each Gospel, but each begins with the same formulation: "Blessed are . . . ," also translated as "Happy are . . ." (Matt 5:1–12;

---

50 Lapsley, 87–88.
51 Lapsley, 90–91.
52 Lapsley, 78, 93.
53 Lapsley, 93.
54 Lapsley, 93.
55 Carl R. Holladay, "The Beatitudes: Happiness and the Kingdom of God," in Strawn, *The Bible and the Pursuit of Happiness*, 141–42.

Luke 6:20–26).[56] The Beatitudes appear at the beginning of a sermon in both Matthew and Luke and serve as moral instructions for Jesus' followers.[57] The purpose of this instruction is to lead the hearers to what Matthew calls the "kingdom of heaven" (Matt 5:3) and what Luke refers to as the "kingdom of God" (Luke 6:20).[58]

Matthew "connects Jesus' vision of happiness with the kingdom of God" and provides "further instruction that illuminates both."[59] The kingdom of God and the happiness or well-being it brings has both present and future dimensions.[60] "Matthew's Jesus locates happiness within the complexity and contradictions" of everyday life and "underscores the enigmatic quality of the blessed life."[61] Biblical scholar Carl R. Holladay provides a concise description of the vision of happiness, one connected to the kingdom of God presented in the Beatitudes.

> One can experience emotions as draining as poverty, whether absolute (Luke) or spiritual (Matthew), as overwhelming and painful as suffering unjustly or as lofty as purified hearts and peacemaking, and yet have all of them named as blessings, with the firm assurance in each case that there is ample warrant for doing so. The overarching promise is that the kingdom of heaven belongs to those at every stage of human experience, high or low, and it is theirs as both promise and fulfillment.[62]

---

56 Holladay, 144.
57 Holladay, 152.
58 Holladay, 153.
59 Holladay, 159.
60 Holladay, 156, 159.
61 Holladay, 160.
62 Holladay, 160.

In this vision of the kingdom of God, flourishing is not something we can ever own fully, but neither is it only a dream in which we participate in some imagined future coming of the kingdom.

Exercise

What biblical passages bring to mind God as happy, joyful, or taking delight in creation and God's people? What biblical passages give us a sense of God's promise to all of creation of flourishing in this life as well as the next?

Theological Reflection on Divine Happiness and Divine Love

As we have seen in our review of select biblical sources, joy and happiness are characteristics of God. Happiness is relational and communal and includes our own happiness. Happiness can include the pleasures of daily life, such as family, enjoyable meals, playfulness, and rejoicing in the gifts of creation.[63] Dimensions of flourishing can be experienced in his life, though we may know it more fully or in a different form in the next. Flourishing involves a way of being in the world in relation to God, others, and self that is characterized by love and made possible by grace. While flourishing does not preclude suffering, because it is a sustained way of being and not a fleeting emotion, it can help us to endure suffering. Flourishing is the point at which "human yearning and Divine fulfillment meet; it is the intersection of hope and help, of desire and gift."[64]

While joy is an important attribute of God that has been overlooked, it is not God's only or primary attribute. Biblical authors in both testaments "consider love a, if not *the,* primary attribute of

---

63 Fretheim, "God, Creation, and the Pursuit of Happiness," 54.
64 William P. Brown, "Happiness and Its Discontents in the Psalms," in Strawn, *The Bible and the Pursuit of Happiness*, 114.

God."[65] The psalmist frequently proclaimed God's "steadfast love," and also describes God's love as "relentless . . . [and] everlastingly loyal."[66] For the psalmist, happiness and joy are grounded in God's goodness, mercy, and love.[67] The biblical witness testifies that divine love promotes the well-being of all creation.[68]

Contributions from Augustine of Hippo

Augustine was one of the first theologians to reflect seriously on a Christian view of happiness. Using popular and familiar philosophical ideas of the day, he constructed a "spiritually compelling Christian philosophy" grounded in scripture.[69] While drawing on Greek ideas familiar to his readers, he avoided "what was incompatible with Christian teaching" and adapted other ideas to develop a Christian teaching that would displace the Greek philosophical view.[70] One of the concepts that Augustine both borrowed and transformed from Greek philosophy was the idea of *eudaomonia*, which refers to happiness as an enduring state of well-being, which accompanies a virtuous life.[71] He sought to provide "a Christian pathway to happiness in God because he believed God wanted us to be happy by living righteously."[72] Augustine's thinking on happiness has significantly influenced Western Christian theology.[73]

Augustine believed that God desires our happiness, which divine grace makes possible. For Augustine, happiness comes

---

65 Oord, *The Nature of Love*, 2.
66 Oord, 2.
67 Brown, "Happiness and Its Discontents in the Psalms," 113.
68 Oord, *The Nature of Love*, 18–19.
69 Charry, *God and the Art of Happiness*, 24.
70 Charry, 24.
71 Strawn, *The Bible and the Pursuit of Happiness*, 15.
72 Charry, *God and the Art of Happiness*, 25.
73 Charry, 24.

from "knowing, loving, and enjoying God and loving self and others in pursuit of that goal."[74] Divine salvation restores our well-being that existed before the fall. But we will only know full happiness in heaven, when "the temptation to sin—that struggle of the self against the self—will end and we will achieve perfect rest in God."[75]

Augustine refuted many of the claims about happiness made by various schools of Greek philosophy popular at the time, particularly Epicureanism, Stoicism, and Neo-Platonism.[76] Some of the philosophical views Augustine sought to refute continue to be influential. Theologian Ellen Charry suggests that an Epicurean view of happiness, which emphasizes enjoyment of the simple pleasures of life, "is closest to the modern secular view."[77] The Greek term associated with this view is *hēdonē*, from which our words *hedonism*, *hedonist*, and *hedonic* come. These Greek philosophical schools believed human beings to be basically good and potentially virtuous, and thought that intentional development and grooming of the innate inner goodness of human beings would form individuals into virtuous citizens.[78] Augustine rejected this view of happiness, finding it incompatible with Christian teaching.[79] However, a belief in an innate human capacity for self-realization, as well as an implied ethical demand for the development of these capacities, continues to be present in contemporary culture.

---

74 Charry, 57.
75 Charry, 60.
76 Charry, 4, 5.
77 Charry, 5.
78 Bjørn Rabjerg, "Evil Understood as the Absence of Freedom: Outlines of a Lutheran Ontology and Anthropology," in Mari-Becker, Dietrich, and Kristian Holm, eds., *What Is Human?*, 197.
79 Charry, *God and the Art of Happiness*, 6.

Healing is a distinctive characteristic of Augustine's doctrine of happiness.[80] Healing, which divine grace makes possible, *is* happiness.[81] This healing comes to us through Christ's incarnation.[82] Ellen Charry thoughtfully articulates Augustine's view of the role of incarnation in our healing: "In becoming human, God takes us into his healing goodness. Salvation is completely the work of God in Christ through grace, and we are genuinely healed of the defect. It seems that incarnation itself is a source of genuine healing in this life."[83] Augustine suggests that happiness comes not only through seeking God, "but that his wisdom, goodness, and beauty actually do heal us to the extent that we know, love, and enjoy him."[84] What is healed in us is "disordered love," which is how Augustine understood sin.[85] While Augustine often referred to sin as pride, what he meant is "badly misshapen self-love."[86] God created us for love, but our love for God, self, and others becomes disordered. God's grace enables the healing of love. Those who are healed through grace can love well, and though this is a lifelong process, "loving well is the basis of a flourishing life"[87]—not success or accolades or even health.

Protestant Views of Happiness

We make a jump now from the Catholic church of the fourth century to the Lutheran Reformation and then to the eighteenth century to consider two Protestant views of well-being. We will

---

80 Charry, 61.
81 Charry, 61.
82 Charry, 61.
83 Charry, 61.
84 Charry, 61.
85 Charry, 157.
86 Charry, 157.
87 Charry, 158.

begin by looking briefly at a key concept in Martin Luther's theology as it contributes to our vision of well-being.

Happiness is probably not the first thing that comes to mind when you think about Martin Luther. I tend to associate Luther with anxiety over salvation, but this is a caricature of his thinking. While Luther seems more concerned with human sinfulness, his vision of Christian freedom can contribute to a theology of happiness.[88] Living in Christ brings justification and freedom.[89] While this is a freedom from "divine wrath," it is also an experience of mercy, which brings joy and healing.[90] Like Augustine, Luther saw Christ's love as healing.[91] Believers are "justified by the Word of God, sanctified made true, peaceful and free, filled with every blessing and truly made a child of God."[92] Luther used the language of "joyful exchange" to describe the process and experience of justification.[93] Through this exchange "the faithful Christian is simultaneously sinner and just," and lives in a "state of dual existence."[94] The soul is still caught in the "burdens and sins of creation," but is moved "beyond earthly care when it experiences the joyous union with God."[95] Freed from fearing God, we are freed to love God, others, and ourselves.

---

88 Charry, 112–13.
89 Charry, 113.
90 Charry, 113.
91 Martin Luther, "The Freedom of a Christian" in Harold J. Grimm, ed., and Helmut T. Lehman, gen. ed., *Luther's Works*, vol. 3, *Career of the Reformer: I* (Philadelphia: Fortress Press, 1957), 349.
92 Luther, "The Freedom of a Christian," 349.
93 Heiko A. Oberman, *Luther: Man Between God and the Devil*, trans. Eileen Walliser-Schwarzbart (New Haven: Yale Univerity Press, 1989), 184.
94 Oberman, 184.
95 Oberman, 184.

John Wesley on Love and Well-Being[96]

Love plays a central role in Wesley's theology. Indeed, Wesley understood divine grace as love and believed that "authentic Christian life flows out of love."[97] Wesley believed that God's love is so extensive and pervasive that it is God's grace that makes us aware of our need for God. Thus, he placed considerable emphasis on prevenient grace, which precedes justifying and sanctifying grace. Influenced by the teaching of the Eastern church, Wesley understood grace as a "co-operant,"[98] meaning that while divine pardoning love is revealed to humanity through the atoning work of Christ, our loving response is made possible through the work of the Holy Spirit. The partnership that grace invites begins with prevenient grace but continues throughout the process of sanctification to salvation. God's prevenient grace makes our response to God's love possible.

Receiving and responding to God's grace creates a bond between us and God and allows us to share in God's nature and be renewed in God's image.[99] Therapeutic metaphors of healing and restoration of health are prominent in Wesley's theology. The human being—body, soul, and spirit—is "infected" with sin, which Wesley compares to "the most fatal leprosy," in his sermon "The One Thing Needful."[100] In his sermon "Original Sin" he declares,

---

96 Some of the material in this section is adapted from Karen D. Scheib, "Love as a Starting Point for Pastoral Theological Refection," *Pastoral Psychology* 63, nos. 5–6 (December 2014): 705–17.

97 Randy Maddox, *Responsible Grace: John Wesley's Practical Theology* (Nashville: Kingswood Books, 1994), 32.

98 Theodore Runyon, *The New Creation: John Wesley's Theology Today* (Nashville: Abingdon Press, 1998), 30.

99 Runyon, 80–81.

100 John Wesley, "The One Thing Needful" in Albert C. Outler and Richard P. Heitzenrater, eds., *John Wesley's Sermons: An Anthology* (Nashville: Abingdon Press, 1987), 35.

"Hereby the great Physician of Souls applies the medicine to heal this sickness, to heal human nature."[101] Wesley understood salvation as a healing of the divine image in us and our capacity to love. As the image of God is renewed in us, so, too, "the happiness that was lost when that image was damaged, is restored.[102] Through salvation we are freed from the bondage of sin and exchange "sickness for health."[103] Grace makes healing possible, and "the happiness that ultimately results from it is a blessing," God's gift to us.[104] Having received the love of God, we are called to grow in grace, which is love, through the process of sanctification.[105]

We see John Wesley's vision of happiness, or flourishing, in his understanding of holiness, both of which are essential to his understanding of salvation.[106] He says that as we grow in love of God, self, and others in the process of sanctification, holiness increases in us. The manifestation of holiness is a life "made more healthy and whole by this communion with God and others.[107] Wesley saw God's redemptive activity as bringing about a new creation. By "faith working in love," God restores "holiness and happiness to all the earth."[108] Wesley viewed the entire arc of the Christian story of creation, fall, and redemption as "an epic with happiness as a central theme."[109] Echoing Augustine, Wesley believed happi-

---

[101] John Wesley, "Original Sin," in Outler and Heitzenrater, *John Wesley's Sermons*, 333.
[102] Sarah Heaner Lancaster, *The Pursuit of Happiness: Blessing and Fulfillment in Chrstian Faith* (Eugene, OR: Wipf & Stock, 2011), 44.
[103] Runyon, *The New Creation*, 80–81.
[104] Lancaster, *The Pursuit of Happiness*, 57.
[105] Runyon, *The New Creation*, 83.
[106] Lancaster, *The Pursuit of Happiness*, 4.
[107] Lancaster, 82.
[108] Lancaster, 169.
[109] E. Brooks Holifield, *Health and Medicine in the Methodist Tradition* (New York: Crossroad, 1986), 64.

ness was found in loving God fully. Holiness included happiness.[110] Because the essence of holiness is love, "love and happiness are tied together," since our true happiness comes about by fulfilling the purpose for which we were created, loving God and others.[111] Because happiness comes about through love, it is more than an inward feeling, and "expresses itself through action," such as works of piety or works of mercy.[112] The more fully our lives fit with God's intention for us to live grounded in love, the more we will experience happiness.[113] Yet happiness does not preclude suffering, nor does suffering negate happiness.[114]

Wesley held that suffering "was not to be sought but to be overcome" and that "the law of love [draws] the Christian into a constant battle against suffering."[115] Wesley manifested this conviction in his care for the poor, his opposition to slavery, "his criticism of prostitution," his concern about alcoholism, and "his worries about hunger in England."[116] When faced with suffering, Wesley was motivated to address the causes of suffering and to see restored the well-being God intended.[117] Wesley saw physical and spiritual well-being as closely connected, and he sought to increase both for all people. Through the classes and bands of the Methodist societies, he provided practices for spiritual growth. He also attended to the physical health of any who sought him out through his practice of medicine and an apothecary (pharmacy).

---

110 Holifield, 64.
111 Lancaster, *The Pursuit of Happiness*, 56, 62.
112 Lancaster, 62.
113 Lancaster, 61. See Lancaster, *The Pursuit of Happiness*, for a fuller discussion of the link between holiness and happiness in John Wesley's theology.
114 Lancaster, 61.
115 Lancaster, 61.
116 Lancaster, 61.
117 Lancaster, 61.

These efforts were short-lived, however, because demand outpaced his ability to provide care to all who needed it. In response, he developed his "Sensible Regimen" and published *The Primitive Physik,* which drew on the best medical texts to offer remedies for common ailments, thus making at least some medical treatments available to those who otherwise had no access to it.[118]

Wesley's theology provides additional grounding for an understanding of flourishing as growth in love. Disordered love is healed through God's grace: God's grace makes it possible for us to grow in our love for God, other, and ourselves. We cannot separate our love for God, self, and others. Some of us may struggle more with loving God, some with loving others, and some with loving ourselves. Growth in love toward flourishing means growing in love in all these dimensions. What God imagines for us and makes possible through grace is flourishing, well-being, life abundant in this life. Flourishing in this life includes physical, mental, spiritual, communal, and societal well-being.

Flourishing Defined (Reprise)

The reflections in this chapter have provided the biblical and theological foundation for a vision of Christian flourishing in this life. I have defined *flourishing* as "a process of dwelling and growing in love of God, self, and other." Divine grace enables growth in love, the fruit of which is moral, spiritual, and psychological healing for individuals, families, and communities and enhanced well-being

---

118 Karen D. Scheib, "1 John Wesley's 'Sensible Regimen: and *Primitive Physik,'"* in *Religion as a Social Determinant of Public Health,* ed. Ellen L. Idler (New York: Oxford University Press, 2014), 114.

of the whole society.[119] Flourishing is intended to be a joyous experience, but does not preclude experiences of suffering. Love accompanies us in suffering so that we can return to the joy God experiences and intends for us. When we are flourishing, we are free to love and care for others because we are freely loved. Love makes flourishing possible.

I hope I have reminded you in this chapter that God desires your happiness, your flourishing well-being. I hope I have borne witness to God's desire for you to grow in love of yourself, as well as others and God, and reminded you that God's grace (and not our own efforts) makes this possible. Growing in love, flourishing in God's love, is a way of being in the world, and it is a lifelong journey. As you continue on this journey, let Julian's vision accompany you: "All shall be well, and all shall be well, and all manner of things shall be well."[120]

Exercise

When do you feel that love is a transaction or that you are obligated to love rather than freed to do so? When do you struggle with feeling responsible for your own perfection or that a desire for flourishing is selfish? What keeps you from participating in the flourishing God intends? What are you holding on to in order to keep you afloat? Can you allow yourself to trust, in the depths of your being, that you are buoyed by God's love? If not, what will it take?

---

119   While I am drawing on Charry's definition here, I have modified it significantly. For her definition of Christian happiness, or what she calls "asherism," see Charry, *God and the Art of Happiness*, xi.
120   Julian of Norwich, *Showings*, 225.

5
Practices for Flourishing

Having a vision of flourishing helps us know where we are headed. But how do we get there? We are formed in the Christian life as we respond to God's grace through participation in spiritual practices, which help attend to God's presence in the world, so that we might grow in love. Spiritual practices affect our whole being, our emotions, our intellect, our relationships, our vocation, our physical health and wellness, as well as our soul or spirit.[1] Our way of being in the world, our sense of vocation, our relationships with others, our relationship with ourselves, as well as how we care for the larger created world are also informed by the habits created through spiritual practices.[2] What we now call spiritual practices are related to what has been traditionally called the means of grace. While this language is less commonly used now, the concept to which it refers continues to play an important role in the Christian tradition. The means of grace are channels through which God's grace is made available to

---

[1] Diane J. Chandler, *Spiritual Formation: An Integrated Approach for Personal and Relational Wholeness* (Downers Grove, IL: IVP Academic, 2014), 18, 19, 21.
[2] Chandler, 21.

us. We tune in to these channels of grace through patterns of living (practices) that form us in the Christian life of love.³

How do we recognize these channels of grace? Wesley believed God provides multiple ways for us to experience grace and gives us a little help by identifying three larger categories of these channels of grace: the *general* means of grace, the *prudential* means of grace, and the *instituted* means of grace. These three categories provide three interrelated avenues through which we might participate in and respond to grace.⁴ We can also identify practices that help us tune in to these different channels of grace.

The first and most broad channel of grace is "the general means of grace," which Wesley thought to be foundational to the other two because they involve our orientation toward God. The general means of grace are about "the inward dispositions of the heart," or all the ways we attend to the presence of God.⁵ The practices associated with this channel of grace include all those that help us pay attention to God, such as centering prayer or contemplative walking. This life orientation of attentiveness to God is the foundation for the "prudential" and "instituted" means of grace.⁶

Recognizing that people will experience God in a number of ways depending on their context and setting, Wesley developed the "category of the prudential means of grace."⁷ Prudence, the root of the word *prudential*, indicates being "wise in practical

---

3   Andrew C. Thompson, *The Means of Grace: Traditioned Practice in Today's World* (Franklin, TN: Seedbed, 2015), 16, 17.
4   Thompson, 18.
5   Thompson, 127, 3.
6   Thompson, 128.
7   Thompson, 101.

affairs."[8] Spiritual practices that fall into this category of grace arise from the "practical wisdom" of everyday life and experience.[9] Wesley recognized the need for developing new spiritual practices of growth in grace relevant to our lives.[10] The first two General Rules fit into the category of prudential means of grace, developed as they were to meet the needs of the emerging Methodist movement and of its members. Wesley's insight in identifying the prudential means of grace gives us the freedom to discover the spiritual practices that work best for us in our context and in our lives. This is good news.

The instituted means of grace are those practices understood as having been instituted by Christ. These practices are found in scripture, belong to the whole church, and are to be observed by all Christians.[11] Wesley specifically names these as: "the public worship of God; the ministry of the Word, either read or expounded; the Supper of the Lord; family and private prayer; searching the scriptures; and fasting or abstinence."[12] Wesley encouraged the regular practice of the instituted means of grace as fundamental to Christian discipleship.[13] If you are in any form of ministry, you may be called upon to lead a congregation in observing "the ordinances of God" following the practices and guidelines of your tradition.

---

8   Dictionary.com, s.v. "prudence," accessed January 9, 2018, http://www.dictionary.com/browse/prudence.
9   Thompson, *The Means of Grace*, 101.
10 Thompson, 101.
11 Henry H. Knight III, *The Presence of God in the Christian Life: John Wesley and the Means of Grace* (Oxford: Scarecrow Press, 1992), 3.
12 John Wesley in Kevin M. Watson, *A Blueprint for Discipleship: Wesley's General Rules as a Guide to Christian Living* (Nashville: Discipleship Resources, 2009), appendix A, "The General Rules," 124–25.
13 Thompson, *The Means of Grace*, 100.

CHAPTER 5

Practicing Love: The General Rules

Practices are "how we actually do things."[14] I define a practice as patterns of behavior and action done over time to meet human needs. One of our human needs is to make meaning, which is a primary purpose of stories. Christian spiritual practices share the basic characteristic of practices by connecting meaning and action, but the meeting of human need occurs "in light of and in response to God's active presence for the life of the world."[15] The intertwining of meaning and action is very clear in religious rituals, which are a specific kind of religious practice. For example, if you walked into a church in the middle of a communion service and did not speak the language of that congregation, you would probably still recognize and understand the actions because you are familiar with the story and the actions used to signal that story. Practices enact a particular story, which communicates certain beliefs, values, and worldview. Through specific Christian practices, we enact God's story of love and flourishing.

The spiritual practices I explore here originate with John Wesley and are part of the Methodist tradition, but I believe they are widely applicable. Soon after the beginning of the Methodist movement, John Wesley developed three guidelines for the members of the Methodist societies, which were a gathering of Wesley's followers divided into smaller groups called bands. These three guidelines, or spiritual practices, are what became known as "The General Rules of the Methodist Societies," or simply "the General Rules," and were intended "to make sure Christianity was

---

14 Karen D. Scheib, *Challenging Invisibility: Practices of Care with Older Women* (St. Louis: Chalice Press, 2004), 50.
15 Dorothy Bass and Craig Dykstra, "A Theological Understanding of Christian Practices, in *Practicing Theology: Beliefs and Practices in Christian Life*, Miroslav Volf and Dorothy Bass, eds. (Grand Rapids: Eerdmans, 2002), 6.

not just a set of beliefs, but that it actually became a way of life."[16] I consider the General Rules as practices for flourishing, because they engage us as whole beings, body, mind, and spirit. Here, I offer a creative interpretation and adaption of Wesley's first two General Rules, which he considered prudential means of grace. Because the prudential means of grace were intended as contextualized practices, they are most amenable to creative adaptation.

Wesley did not design these rules as a yardstick to judge the quality of a person's faith, but rather to provide a way to grow in grace and love. At the heart of Wesley's theology is the deep conviction of God's abundant, generous, voluminous love—that is, grace. Wesley said that the nature of grace *is* love. Grace makes it possible for us to follow the Christian life, and to increase our love of God, others, and ourselves. The General Rules are embedded in Wesley's understanding of grace and salvation, and are lived out in community. Community members who participated in the Methodist societies during Wesley's time were expected to follow these rules to show their desire for salvation.[17] The Rules provided guidance for living one's faith in daily life in response to God's transforming grace. Said more simply: Wesley provided the General Rules to help us respond to God's grace and grow in love. The theological term we use for that is *sanctification*. These Rules and the practices they suggest likewise help us increase our love of God, self, and others today.

Three "Rules"

The Rules or practices sound simple, and there are only three: (1) Do no harm, (2) Do good, (3) Attend [to] all the ordinances of

---

16 Watson, *A Blueprint for Discipleship*, 11.
17 Watson, 52.

CHAPTER 5

God.[18] The first two, which Wesley considered prudential means of grace, seem rather clear. Wesley's hearers would have understood the third one, but the language is definitely eighteenth-century! Methodist historian Kevin Watson translates the third rule as "practice spiritual disciplines," though Wesley had some very specific disciplines in mind, which fell under the category of instituted means of grace.[19] Another way to think about "ordinances of God" is in terms of the practices that help us know God better, such as reading scripture, prayer, and partaking in the Lord's Supper. All the practices listed under the third rule are both embodied, and some, particularly worship and the sacraments, are communal practices.

When considering the General Rules, we need to recall that the original purpose for which these guidelines were developed was for spiritual formation in small groups. In the early Methodist movement, these groups took the form of bands, classes made up primarily of laypeople, who were also members of the Church of England. In the third General Rule, Wesley reminds his followers to participate in the corporate worship of the church, as well as the smaller groups. When Wesley encouraged the practice of receiving the Lord's Supper, not only weekly, but as often as possible, he expected his followers to do so in the Anglican Church.[20]

The intention of all three of Wesley's General Rules is to provide a foundation for growth in love of God, self, and other. Loving God with all our hearts, minds, and souls is the greatest commandment. In Matthew 22:34–36 we find some religious leaders

---

18 *The Book of Discipline of The United Methodist Church*, 2012, UMC.org, accessed January 9, 2018, http://www.umc.org/what-we-believe/general-rules-of-the-methodist-church.
19 Watson, *A Blueprint for Discipleship*, 11.
20 See John Wesley, "The Duty of Constant Communion," in Thomas Jackson, ed., *The Works of John Wesley*, repr. ed. (Grand Rapids: Zondervan, 1958), 3:429.

trying to trap Jesus by asking him, "Teacher, which commandment in the law is the greatest?"[21] He answers that loving God is the greatest commandment, but there is a second important commandment: "Love your neighbor as yourself."[22] Jesus understood that these commandments were inseparable. Love for God, other, and ourselves are intertwined. Because sometimes we need help understanding what loving God, neighbor, and self looks like, Jesus elaborates. In the parable of the good Samaritan, he describes neighbor love, and the Gospels say a lot about loving God. The practices Wesley recommends are couched in language that similarly focuses on love of God and other. In my creative reflection on the General Rules I primarily consider how these guidelines might help us grow in proper love of self.

Considering Self-Love

Perhaps Jesus and Wesley assumed that we love ourselves enough. But in my experience as a pastor, pastoral counselor, and teacher of pastoral care, not only have I struggled with loving myself enough; I have also encountered many people who struggle with loving themselves in the way God intends. Though they try to love God and others, both tasks prove difficult—probably because they aren't loving themselves too. This was true of a church member I'll call Sally. Though she could recite John 3:16, she believed God's love did not apply to her, that she was fundamentally unlovable, by others and even by God. Not surprisingly, though she tried to love others, she could never trust anyone fully because she did not believe their love for her could be genuine since she was unlovable. Lack of proper self-love can get in the way of loving others and God.

---

21 Matthew 22:36 NRSV.
22 Matthew 22:39 NRSV.

What is considered proper self-love has been a contentious issue in Christian theology. On one side of the debate a proper form of self-love is considered possible and encouraged, though theologians present various views of what this looks like in actual practice. On the other side of the debate is a suspicion that any form of self-love is corrupted by sin and is only an expression of self-interest.[23] We receive a mixed message even in scripture. Jesus includes love of self in the second commandment, which suggests that self-love is possible and necessarily connected to loving God and others. On the other hand, the author of 2 Timothy warns us against people who are "lovers of themselves" but "not lovers of the good" (2 Tim 3:2, 3b), meaning someone who is self-absorbed and is concerned with no one else. As a result of such different biblical testimonies, many of us might be confused. Is self-love acceptable or sinful? Christian theologians have taken up both sides of this debate.[24]

The side of the debate suspicious of self-love has significantly influenced Protestant theology.[25] This theological position holds that self-love should be "rigorously suppressed in favor of the love of God and neighbor."[26] It says that to love others as ourselves is not about self-love at all; it means we should extend to our neighbor the same concern we have for ourselves.[27] This view of self-love can move us to an idea that our love for God and others should be selfless and self-sacrificial and that any form of self-concern is selfish.[28] Many of us have inherited this theological position with-

---

[23] Sondra Wheeler, *What We Were Made For: Christian Reflections on Self-Love* (San Francisco: Jossey-Bass, 2007), 94.
[24] Wheeler, 94.
[25] Wheeler, 94.
[26] Wheeler, 94.
[27] Wheeler, 94.
[28] Wheeler, 94.

out knowing that it is only one side of the debate within the larger Christian tradition. If we are operating with this view of self-love as suspect, or a form of sin, and love for others as self-sacrificial, it is not surprising that we are ambivalent about self-care. In fact, clergy in the Duke study reported this ambivalence.[29]

Exercise

How do you regard self-love? What teachings or traditions have shaped your view? What do you get out of holding on to this view?

Redefining Self-Love

Before we can engage in practices that express proper self-love, we need a different story about love of self. One step in discovering a different theological story is to recover voices in the Christian tradition that see the love of God, others, and self as intertwined and inseparable, rather than subordinating love of self to love of others. Another step is to develop a more complex view of what distorts love (what defines sin). Following through completely on both of these steps is a huge task; here I offer only a brief sketch, starting with the second point.

Christian theology has tended to distort self-love as being excessive or prideful. More recently, theologians have deemed "excessive self-abnegation" to be sinful.[30] Sin is whatever separates us from God. Being absorbed with self-loathing or self-doubt can separate us from God as much as being absorbed with self-love.

---

29 Duke Clergy Health Initiative, Summary Report, 2014 Statewide Survey of United Methodist Clergy in North Carolina, https://divinity.duke.edu/sites/divinity.duke.edu/files/documents/chi/2014%20Summary%20Report%20-%20CHI%20Statewide%20Survey%20of%20United%20Methodist%20Clergy%20in%20North%20Carolina%20-%20web.pdf.

30 Darlene Fozard Weaver, *Self-Love and Christian Ethics* (Cambridge, UK: Cambridge University Press, 2002), 62.

Some feminist theologians have demonstrated how religious, cultural, and social expectations have shaped women to be far more prone to self-abnegation than to pride.[31] This was Sally's story. The stories she'd inherited about women's roles and place had shaped her to ignore her own needs. She thought of herself as unworthy of God's love, and her lack of self-love kept her separated from God and others. In my experience, women are not the only ones who suffer from lack of self-love, but they have over centuries of enculturation unfortunately become particularly adept at it. Just as we cannot love God without loving others, I believe we cannot love God properly if we don't love ourselves.

So what does it look like to love ourselves as God intends? I turn to the work of several contemporary theologians for help here.[32] Instead of understanding love of self as primarily self-sacrificial, Thomas Jay Oord asserts that "loving ourselves for our own sake has a proper role in the Christian life."[33] Love, as Oord defines it, is "to act intentionally, in sympathetic/empathic response to God and others, to promote overall well-being."[34] This definition of love is intended to be descriptive of both divine and human love and "to account for all actions we should genuinely call loving."[35] Love that intentionally "promot[es] overall well-being" is grounded in the common testimony of the Old Testament and the New Testament.[36] If God's love seeks to promote the well-being of all, and we are called to "imitate divine love, we ought to love

---

31 Weaver, 62.
32 See, for one example, Weaver.
33 Thomas Jay Oord, *The Nature of Love: A Theology* (St. Louis: Chalice Press, 2010), 81.
34 Oord, 17.
35 Oord, 17.
36 Oord, 18.

ourselves so as to promote our own well-being."[37] Well-being may require moments or acts of self-sacrifice, "but love is not always self-sacrificial."[38]

Running throughout the Christian tradition is the conviction that God is the source of love.[39] In the classic tradition (represented by Augustine, among others), God is the highest good. As we are drawn to God through grace, we flourish.[40] As I love God properly and fully, I am able to love God and my neighbor as God intends.[41] As we open ourselves to the fullness of God's love, and love God more fully in response, we are drawn both outward toward our neighbor, and inward toward the image of God being restored in us through grace. We cannot love God fully if we love our neighbors less than we love ourselves or if we love ourselves less than we love our neighbors.[42]

Exercise

We often think we must move from loving God to loving others, and only then to loving ourselves. Think of another person you have a hard time loving. Now think of an aspect or part of yourself you have a hard time loving. Imagine this other person through God's loving eyes. Imagine yourself though God's loving eyes.

---

37 Oord, 81.
38 Oord, 82.
39 Werner G. Jeanrond, *A Theology of Love* (London: T&T Clark, 2010), 30.
40 Weaver, *Self-Love and Christian Ethics*, 3.
41 Gene Outka, "Universal Love and Impartiality," in Edmund N. Santurri and William Werpehowski, eds. *The Love Commandments: Essays in Christian Ethics and Moral Philosophy* (Washington, DC: Georgetown University Press, 1992), 2.
42 Outka, 3. I have given a rather simple summary of Outka's claims regarding the relationship between love of God, self, and neighbor. His argument is complex and based on concepts of the universality and impartiality of God's love.

What difference might it make in how we respond to others if we see ourselves as well as others through God's loving eyes?

Playing by (with) the General Rules

I believe a creative adaptation of Wesley's General Rules, particularly the first two, can guide us toward proper self-love through doing no harm to ourselves; doing good to our bodies, minds, and souls; and engaging in the spiritual practices that help us grow in grace. If you look up "The General Rules," you will note that Wesley has a list of examples or sub-points under each one to show what each rule looks like in practice.[43] Since his language is a bit dated, his examples can seem somewhat harsh. This is where our creativity and playfulness comes in.

When we play, we are usually trying something out, or putting together things that don't seem to go together. We often think of play as something only children do, something we put away along with other childish things when we become adults. Yet in reality, to be a playful person has more to do with our attitudes, how we look at things, than with specific activities.[44] Pastoral theologian Jaco Hamman suggests that the capacity to play is a sign of maturity and an essential capacity for pastors.[45] Playfulness, which requires imagination, can lead to seeing things differently and can make growth and transformation possible.[46] God's playfulness is seen throughout Scripture. Sarah laughs when she hears God will grant

---

43 "The General Rules of the Methodist Church," UMC.org, accessed January 9, 2018, http://www.umc.org/what-we-believe/the-general-rules-of-the-methodist-church.

44 Jaco Hamman, *On Becoming a Pastor: Forming Self and Soul for Ministry, Revised and Updated* (Cleveland: Pilgrim Press, 2014), 177.

45 Hamman, 174–75.

46 Hamman, 174.

her a baby in old age (Gen 18:9–14). Nicodemus can't imagine how he might be born again, but God can (John 3:1–10). A creative, playful adaptation of the General Rules can help us imagine new ways to grow in love for ourselves, others, and God.

The first two General Rules fall into the category of prudential means of grace and are more appropriate for creative adaptation. The third General Rule deals with the instituted means of grace, which includes worship and the sacraments. Since most denominations have well-established practices regarding worship and the celebration of the sacraments, I am not offering a creative adaptation of these practices. In the next chapter I do consider how writing as a spiritual practice can be a form of prayer, which is considered one of the "ordinances of God," and falls under the third General Rule.

Do No Harm

"By doing no harm, by avoiding evil of every kind, especially that which is most generally practiced . . ."[47]

The first Wesleyan practice that we'll examine is "doing no harm."[48] Harm is anything that interferes in our relationship with God; thwarts our growth in love of God, self, or other; and inhibits flourishing of any and all. Wesley gives specific examples of what he considers harm, and his list is shaped by the historical era in which he wrote it. One of Wesley's examples of harm is a reverse version of the Golden Rule: "Doing to others as we would not they should do unto us" (meaning, don't do something to others you don't want them to do to you).[49]

---

[47] "The General Rules of the Methodist Church.
[48] "The General Rules."
[49] "The General Rules."

CHAPTER 5

On Not Harming Bodies

Wesley was quite concerned with the welfare of bodies. When Wesley gave specific examples of "doing no harm," he referred to the way we treat others' bodies. We are not to do violence to them, or to treat anyone as less than human, or to see bodies as a commodity for sale.[50] Wesley was very concerned about preserving and restoring the health of his followers because he considered health a gift from God, and a gift to be treated with care.[51] He expressed this idea of health as a divine gift, which requires our stewardship, in his sermon "The Good Steward" (1768): "We are not at liberty to use what he has lodged in our hands as we please, but as he pleases."[52] God has given us the gift of our marvelous, complex bodies, and often imperfect bodies. In response, we treat this gift with care. Maintaining our health is not the ultimate goal or a moral obligation as in the "wellness syndrome"; it simply means tending and caring for the precious gift we have received.

The harm we may do to our bodies will be different for each one of us. Some forms of behavior that can cause serious harm to our bodies, such as addiction, eating disorders, or self-cutting, may not begin as intentional forms of harm. Such behaviors may be driven by a variety of factors. In some cases, such behaviors are responses to deep wounds, including physical, sexual, or emotional abuse as children. In these behaviors, the harm once suffered as a child is internalized along with a message that "I am not good enough" or "I deserve to be punished," a message often perpetuated by deep feelings of shame. Underneath may be an experience

---

50 "The General Rules." See specific prohibition against slavery.
51 Scheib, "Christian Commitment to Public Well-Being," 121 (see chap. 4, n. 118).
52 Wesley, "The Good Steward," *Works*, 6:138, cited in Ott, "John Wesley on Health," 198.

of betrayal of love or a feeling of being damaged and unlovable. Repairing these forms of harm requires long-term intervention, and usually professional psychological as well as spiritual care.

We may not see some of the behaviors in which we engage as self-harm, though we might think we could take better care of ourselves. The forms of self-harm in which we engage are often more ordinary, unintentional, and sometimes socially acceptable. Overwork, perfectionism, and self-criticism are behaviors in which many of us engage. But if these behaviors get in the way of loving God, others, or self, they may cause us harm. Each one of us will have to identify the small, everyday ways we do harm to ourselves, because they will be as unique to us as our stories. Because suggestions for clergy self-care have often focused on care of our bodies, let's look at some of the ways our bodies suffer from lack of self-love. I have to admit that I often don't take as good care of the gift of my body as I might.

I have a tendency to ignore the messages my body is sending me. I imagine I'm not the only one who does this. We ignore bodily cues that we are exhausted and power through, staying up all night to finish a work project, to write a paper for school, to work on a sermon, to check one more thing off our to-do list, or to help a child with a school assignment. When I have set a deadline for myself on a writing project, I often have a compulsion to meet the deadline, even if it means pushing myself too hard. Much of the time, my deadline is self-created, meaning nothing is significantly lost if I don't meet it, except the image of myself as a person who gets things done. As a result, I often sit for hours at a time, ending up stiff and sore and resorting to medication to ease that pain. To do no harm in this context might mean that I set a timer for twenty minutes and make myself get up and move, releasing the pressure on my spine and reducing my chronic back pain. Most of us can get away with that once in a while, but the body has ways of getting our attention.

Exercise

Jot down some of the messages your body sends that you ignore. What are some of the socially acceptable behaviors you engage in (overwork, not getting enough sleep, etc.) that may be causing you harm?

On Witnessing to *the Savior, Not* Being *the Savior*

Included under "doing no harm" Wesley cautioned against "[d]oing what we know is not for the glory of God," and then gave examples.[53] Many of these examples don't fit our contemporary setting, but I think we can interpret this phrase in a way that makes sense to us, such as that I can get confused between bearing witness to the Savior and being the savior. Both Barbara Brown Taylor and Jonathan Martin confessed to such confusion, or temptation. We get caught in this confusion when we begin to believe that saving others is up to us—doing the work of temporarily righting someone else's relationships rather than helping him understand and correct the fundamental imbalance and injustice in it; fixing a child's, colleague's, or student's paper or assignment instead of pushing her to learn to do it herself; or swooping in to a situation of injustice and poverty overseas, fixing it in the short term, but not recognizing how our own lifestyles contribute to the underlying power imbalances.

Faced with significant human suffering, the compassionate response is to do something. Being present and loving the people in our care often feels as though it is not enough. Students want to right the wrongs and correct the injustices in institutions

---

53 "The General Rules of the Methodist Church."

and society in the fifteen weeks of the semester. And they have a point. We are called not only to mercy but also to justice. What is sometimes hard to remember is that we are partnering with God in the healing work already under way. But it is very easy, especially in a culture that praises individual achievement, to believe that it is all up to us and we are personally responsible. When it's all going well, it feels great and we can begin to believe that we can save the world. But when we burn out, as Barbara Brown Taylor and I did, or pilot our ship onto the rocks, as Martin describes, we realize we cannot do it all ourselves. This is a lesson we rarely learn the first time. It seems to be part of the human struggle to want to be in control, to be God-like, rather than to be a creature reflecting the divine image. Loving ourselves means leaning into that reality.

A complicating factor in challenging our overly high expectations of ourselves is that congregations occasionally reinforce these expectations. Do we look at the way congregations or denominations may unintentionally encourage a savior complex by holding clergy personally responsible for the success or failure of a congregation? We often encourage clergy to avoid burnout by participating in practices of individual self-care, such as eating right, exercising, and reducing stress through spiritual practices. Yet congregations or a denomination frequently encourage and reward practices of ministry that lead to burnout while holding clergy responsible for their self-care. If we are to hold together love of God, self, and others, we must take into account the communal, social, and institutional factors that thwart our flourishing.

Exercise

Do you struggle with wanting to fix or solve others' problems? If so, can you identify what is most likely to trigger this behavior in you? Do you ever feel that expectations from your congregation trigger this behavior? Is there anything in your own story that contributes to a desire to fix or take care of others?

Avoid Uncharitable or Unprofitable Conversations

Under the rubric of "do no harm" Wesley advised his followers to avoid participating in uncharitable or unprofitable conversations.[54] His primary focus was not talking about others in these ways, and this, too, is good advice. Let's consider, though, what it might mean to not engage in uncharitable or unprofitable conversations with ourselves. I imagine I am not the only one who focuses on the one negative comment on an evaluation form while ignoring the many positive statements. Probably much like yours, my inner critic engages in uncharitable conversation about me: "I can't believe I did that; I am so stupid." Or, "I'll never get that promotion. I am not good enough." Or "If I can't get an A, I must be dumb. Why bother trying?"

All of us have an inner critic. The ability to evaluate our behavior honestly is a part of being a mature adult. Jesus reminds us to remove the logs from our own eyes before we worry about the speck in another's eye (Matt 7:3). Hopefully, we also have an inner cheerleader that encourages us and says, "Way to go!" that praises our strengths and capacities. Most of the time, the voices of our inner critic and inner cheerleader sound a lot like our parents' voices. But for some of us, for a variety of complex reasons, our inner critic grows to huge proportions and our cheerleader shrinks to a tiny size. The reasons for this imbalance are often rooted in our childhood and how we experienced our parents, which may or may not be a full or accurate depiction. After all, we're children when we form impressions of our parents, and we don't yet have a

---

54 "The General Rules."

fair and complete picture of them as human beings. In any event, some of us reach adulthood with very loud and vocal inner critics.

Other voices outside of ourselves that become internalized also feed our inner critic. The master narratives of our culture, which often convey ideas about race, gender roles, age, sexuality, and attitudes toward bodies, are often communicated through the narrative environments of family, school, or church and can "significantly shape our sense of self."[55] Oppressive voices that tell us we are less and that attempt to keep us in place by social practices of discrimination based on race or gender can become so internalized that they cause significant harm by rendering us invisible. Pastoral theologian Greg Ellison eloquently captures the devastating consequence of invisibility as being "cut dead but still alive."[56] While Ellison specifically looks at how young African Americans are "cut dead," this state of being applies to any individual groups who are marginalized and rendered disposable and invisible.[57] Invisibility leads to muteness as external forces refuse to acknowledge another's existence or hear their cries.[58] Imposed silence can render a person "mute" and force an "internal silencing," leading to "an incapacity or unwillingness" to express our internal thoughts and feelings.[59] Invisibility is a form of imposed self-abnegation and is contrary to love. Doing no harm means acknowledging, interrupting, and resisting the muteness and invisibility imposed on others and ourselves.

The practice of doing no harm can tell us what kinds of behaviors to avoid or describe the consequences of harm, which some of

---

55 Scheib, *Pastoral Care*, 85.
56 Gregory C. Ellison III, *Cut Dead but Still Alive: Caring for African American Young Men* (Nashville: Abingdon Press, 2013), 1.
57 Ellison, 1.
58 Ellison, 3.
59 Ellison, 3.

us know all too well. One of Wesley's keen insights is that avoiding harm is not necessarily the same as doing good. This takes us to Wesley's second practice.

Exercise

How would you estimate the size of your inner critic (big, medium, small)? Write down some of the phrases your inner critic most often says to you? How do you respond to these statements?

Do Good

"By doing good; by being in every kind merciful after their power; as they have opportunity, doing good of every possible sort, and, as far as possible, to all."[60]

Wesley's second guideline is generally expressed in two words: "do good." For Wesley, at the heart of doing good is mercy: to "do good" is to be merciful. *Merriam-Webster's Dictionary* defines being merciful as "treating people with kindness and forgiveness," being "compassionate."[61] *Compassion* is a synonym for mercy. In Luke 6:36 we read, "Be merciful, just as your Father is merciful" (NIV). The New Living Translation says it this way: "You must be compassionate, just as your Father is compassionate." Resisting the forces that would render us invisible are acts of mercy and compassion as well as acts of justice. Since Ellison details the process of caring for those who are rendered mute and invisible and "cut dead,"[62] my focus here is on the inner critic who can be tricked into colluding with external voices that tell us we are not good enough. We can develop practices of self-compassion and develop narratives

---

60 "The General Rules."
61 Merriam-Webster.com, s.v. "merciful," accessed January 9, 2018, http://www.merriam-webster.com/dictionary/merciful.
62 See Ellison, *Cut Dead but Still Alive*, for his discussion on resisting invisibility and caring for those who are "cut dead."

of resistance against internal and external voices that diminish our sense of worth and well-being.

Self-Compassion

If you have ever tried to argue with your inner critic, you've already discovered that this rarely works well. Psychologist Kristin Neff develops a practice of self-compassion as a way of quieting our inner critics and lessening self-judgment.[63] Can you be as kind and compassionate to yourself as you are to others? I continue to struggle with this. If I am lucky, a good friend will prompt me into such self-loving behavior by asking me, "What would you say to someone else in this situation? Can you say this to yourself?" Neff says that "having compassion for ourselves is no different than having compassion for others."[64]

The three components of self-compassion that Neff identifies are "self-kindness, common humanity, and mindfulness" or non-judgmental awareness.[65] The first step toward compassion—self-kindness—means to notice suffering and be moved by it.[66] Before we can respond compassionately to our pain, we must recognize it.[67] While some forms of pain are hard to ignore, Neff suggests that we often ignore the particular pain that comes from self-judgment when we come up against limitations or feel we have failed.[68] Having "self-compassion means [we] are kind and

---

63 Kristin Neff, *Self-Compassion: Stop Beating Yourself Up and Leave Insecurity Behind* (New York: William Morrow, Harper Collins, 2011).
64 Kristin Neff, "Definition of Self-Compassion" Self-Compassion, accessed January 9, 2018, http://self-compassion.org/the-three-elements-of-self-compassion-2/.
65 Neff, *Self-Compassion*, 41.
66 Neff, 10.
67 Neff, 10.
68 Neff, "Definition of Self-Compassion."

understanding" rather than judgmental when we fail to meet our expectations.[69] Self-kindness notices our suffering and allows us to be "gentle and understanding with ourselves rather than harshly critical."[70]

To acknowledge our common humanity is to accept that we are just as human as the next person and that we are not alone in experiencing suffering. It reminds us that we are creatures and not the creator: we are not all-knowing or all-seeing; we will make mistakes; we will bump up against our limitations.

The third element of self-compassion is "mindfulness," or a balanced awareness.[71] Awareness is the capacity to observe our emotional reactions without judgment. Developing this capacity takes time. Any form of contemplative prayer, like centering prayer, can help us become more aware of what we are thinking and feeling and simply observe, "Oh, I am feeling sad now." This does not mean the sadness, or anger, or whatever the feeling is will immediately go away, but we may be able to be more accepting of it and ourselves and be kind to ourselves in the meantime.

Yet what often happens is that we don't notice or pay regard to our own pain, and instead of being kind to ourselves, we connect the pain with a feeling *we think we should not have,* like anger. We then judge ourselves for having that feeling and try to push it away. Most of the time the feeling pushes back, and the next thing we know, we are lost in the feeling. An unwelcome insight that came to me in the process of learning to be more self-compassionate is the recognition that the harsh judgment I level against myself can sometimes be leveled against others. I believe that increasing our compassion for ourselves increases our compassion for others.

---

69 Neff.
70 Neff.
71 Neff, *Self-Compassion*, 41.

Likewise, awareness of the depth of compassion we can have for others can increase our compassion for ourselves. I have found the three steps of self-compassion to be a way to "do good" in my own life.[72]

Exercise

Try practicing the three steps of self-compassion. Go back to one of the phrases your inner critic commonly says. Are you aware of the pain this causes? Can you notice and acknowledge the pain? Can you acknowledge that you are not the only one who sometimes messes up? What would you say to a friend who is feeling the kind of pain you are feeling? What kind and compassionate words might you say to yourself?

Narratives of Resistance

While practices of self-compassion may help quiet our inner critic, narratives of resistance can push back against the demeaning external voices that become internalized. Narratives of resistance emerge when individuals and communities claim the authority to tell their own life stories and refuse social definitions and practices that render them invisible.[73] As a Christian practice, narratives of resistance reflect the theological insistence on the divine worth of all God's people. We see a communal example of narratives of resistance linked to the Christian narrative in the civil rights movement. Leaders like Martin Luther King Jr. and Howard Thurman acted from a deep belief that God is a loving and liberating God who desires freedom for all of God's people. This belief formed their call for a change in the American treatment of African

---

72 For a more detailed discussion of these practices, see Neff, *Self-Compassion*.
73 See Scheib, *Challenging Invisibility*, 143, for an earlier formulation of this definition.

Americans, which included freedom from the institutional powers, such as the Jim Crow laws in the South or the less formalized, but still powerful racism in other parts of the United States.

Individuals may also give shape to their own distinctive narratives of resistance. In my research with older women, I discovered many individual examples of such narratives of resistance, and many were rejections of negative social stereotypes of aging, such as when Kate advised young pastors working with older adults: "Forget age. That is not important. We have got to erase the idea that age makes a difference."[74] Her narrative of resistance was to reject the notion that she was defined primarily by her age, rather than her gifts as a person, regardless of age. Courage may be required to push against the external stories others impose on us and create narratives of resistance to diminish the negative spiritual, psychological, and physical effects of marginalization and invisibility.

Exercise

Have you had to form your own narratives of resistance to push back imposed invisibility or others' stereotypical views of you? How do you nurture and sustain these narratives?

Honoring the Body: Preserving Health Through Preventative Care

As we saw earlier, Wesley reminds us that health is a gift from God and that God desires our physical as well as spiritual well-being. Five years after the General Rules were published, Wesley published *The Primitive Physik,* "a small, inexpensive tract that made the best current medical knowledge available to people" who had

---

74 Scheib, 143.

little access to physicians or medical care.[75] While most of *The Primitive Physik* is filled with remedies for treating various illnesses and restoring health, Wesley was also concerned about preserving the health of his followers. Tending the gift of health required discipline to maintain it.[76] Maintaining the gift of health we have received from God requires responsibility and discipline.[77] While "Wesley articulated his concern for the prevention of illness in his sermons," he laid out guidelines for maintaining health, or his "sensible regimen," in the preface to *The Primitive Physik*.[78] Here is an excerpt:

> Observe at all times the greatest exactness in your regimen or manner of living. Abstain from all mixed, all high-seasoned food. Use plain diet, easy of digestion; and this sparingly as you can, consistent with ease and strength. Drink only water, if it agrees with your stomach, if not, good clean small beer. Use as much exercise daily in the open air, as you can without weariness. Sup at six or seven, on the lightest food; go to bed early and rise betimes. To persevere with steadiness in this course is more than half the cure. Above all, add to the rest, (for it is not labor lost) that old fashionable medicine, prayer. And have faith in God who *killeth and maketh alive, who bringeth down to the grave and bringeth up*.[79]

We hear Wesley advocating what "we would now consider preventive health practices," though in eighteenth-century language.[80]

---

75   Scheib, "Christian Commitment to Public Well-Being," 114.
76   Scheib, 121.
77   Scheib, 121.
78   Scheib, 121.
79   John Wesley, preface to *The Primitive Physic,* cited in Deborah Madden, *"A Cheap, Safe and Natural Medicine": Religion, Medicine, and Culture in John Wesley's "Primitive Physik"* (Amsterdam: Rodopi B.V., 2007), 155.
80   Scheib, "Christian Commitment to Public Well-Being," 121.

His advice seems remarkably similar to the current advice for clergy self-care: exercise, eat right, and reduce stress. The difference for Wesley is that health was seen as something worth preserving and increasing, but only as was a part of the ultimate good of salvation. Caring for bodies is integral to Wesley's holistic understanding of salvation, which encompasses soul *and* body.[81] Practices of tending to bodies "were deeply embedded in the life of the Methodist movement and evident in the practices of the classes and societies."[82] Perhaps it is time we reclaimed these practices of attending to bodies, including our own, not for the sake of wellness itself, but as a loving response to God's care for us.

The good news is that the General Rules are guidelines to a process. Growth in love, or sanctification, likewise is a process. We won't get it right the first time. In the early church, it was common for those in the procession during the mass to perform a particular step, known as the *tripudium*, as they moved through the sanctuary. This step had three parts: two steps forward and one back. It was a reminder of the reality of the Christian life: though we are moving forward, our progress is not constant. This is the reality of the human condition; grace moves us forward, and we step back.

Exercise

What spiritual practices do you have that allow for you to attend to yourself? In what ways can you make room for yourself so that you can attend to your physical and emotional health? What difference would it make if caring for your body felt less like an "ought" and more like a response to God's gifts of body and health?

---

81 Scheib, 116.
82 Scheib, 116.

Expanding Our Spiritual Practices

Through our playful consideration of the General Rules, we have expanded our notions of Christian practices beyond the usual list—of public and private prayer, worship, communion, and searching the scriptures (the instituted means of grace)—to include self-compassion, narratives of resistance, and honoring the body. Other scholars have expanded the list as well, adding keeping Sabbath, friendship, and peacemaking, among others.[83] Through exercising our "practical wisdom," we are free to discover and claim the practices that work best for us in promoting our spiritual growth.[84] You may already be engaged in practices that serve as channels of grace for you, but you perhaps never fully realized this because it did not fit your stereotype of what spiritual practice looks like.

Guess what? You can make your own list. Through exercising practical wisdom, you can discover or develop the spiritual practices that work best to foster growth in love and flourishing. Perhaps looking through the lens of a camera helps you see God's presence in the world differently. Or maybe the repetitive click-clacking of knitting needles, or the rhythmic fall of an ax while splitting wood, is your meditation, heightening your awareness of God's presence. Spiritual practices can take many forms, but share a common purpose. Writing has become my spiritual practice. Whatever form spiritual practices take, they move us toward the same goal: "to be aware and awake, open to God, ourselves, and the world around us" so that we may be transformed."[85]

---

83 See Practicing Faith, http://www.practicingourfaith.org, for a list of resources and books on Christian practices (accessed January 9, 2018).
84 Practicing Faith.
85 Helen Cepero, *Journaling as a Spiritual Practice: Encountering God Through Attentive Writing* (Downers Grove, IL: InterVarsity Press, 2008), 12.

6
Writing as Spiritual Practice and Story Care

August 9, 2017: Journal Entry

Rivendell, Sewanee, TN

I am sitting on a rock overlooking Lost Cove and the treed ridges of the Cumberland Plateau. The sun has just climbed over the top of the hills. I've come here to talk to God. The creek is full again after the rain and I hear the brook happily tumbling over the rocks to the pool below. I hear a crow cawing, the crickets' steady hum, and the complex melodic song of the goldfinch. A hawk flies above and lands in the trees behind me. I am listening.

I sigh. Sometimes, Holy One, I don't know how to talk to you. As I sit in the beauty of your creation, I am amazed by your majesty, so I call you Holy One. Yet that leaves me feeling you are so high, I cannot attain you. I want to feel you close by, like a good friend sitting with me in silence. I pull myself away from my thoughts of my inadequacy to pay attention to what I see, hear, smell and feel. I focus my attention on the emerald leaf in front of me, hold it in my hand and feel its slick surface. Suddenly, I am aware the leaf is coursing with life, though at a pace slower than I can observe. The sweet earthy smell of wet grass comes to me on the breeze as does the big bold song of the little Carolina Wren.

I sat down on the lichen-covered rock wanting to reach out for you God, wanting to touch the edge of your heavenly garment. I realize now that I am swathed in holy presence. I am no longer just looking at the trees, woods, and hills around me, I feel a part of them now. I am reminded of a line from a poem by Rumi, "this longing you express is the return message."[1] Thank you, Holy One, for your nearness this morning.

I wrote this journal entry while in the Tennessee mountains, finishing this book. Early morning is my preferred time to write, before my mind is cluttered with the list of things to do for the day. I might have had the same experience of prayer without writing my thoughts down. In fact, I first sat on the rock without my journal, but quickly realized that my thoughts were swirling. I find that writing helps me slow down, organize my thoughts, and focus my attention. I also had the sense that I wanted to hold on to something about this moment, some awareness that I might want to come back to and reflect on it more deeply, so I ran and got my journal.

When writing is a part of my spiritual practice, I don't pay attention to grammar, or spelling, or sentence structure. I just write what comes to me. Sometimes, I am scribbling so fast I have

---

1 Jalaluddin Mevlana Rumi, "Love Dogs," GoodReads, accessed January 9, 2018, https://www.goodreads.com/quotes/109002-love-dogs-one-night-a-man-was-crying-allah-allah.

trouble later making out what I have said. I don't worry much about the quality of my writing because it is the process that is most important. Most of my journal entries are written for myself and are not intended for publication, including this piece.[2] However, it only seems fair since I am asking you to give writing a try as a spiritual practice that I share my process and writing with you. Even though I worry the pieces are not my best writing, they are a part of my spiritual journey and therefore important to me.

Writing, primarily journaling, has been an important practice throughout much of my life. My journal provides a place for me to try and make sense of things that make no sense, and to express my hopes, fears, grief, and prayers. While writing always seemed something I needed to do for my well-being, it was not until I expanded my imagination about what might function as a spiritual practice that I was able to claim writing as my practice. Writing is the spiritual practice that has been reliable for me and to which I continually turn. Writing is also a practice well suited to story care and the related processes of close reading and restorying. Writing as a spiritual practice can also help connect our life stories to God's story of flourishing. In this chapter, I explore how writing as a spiritual practice contributes to story care.

Exercise

Write a short letter to God. What's on your mind right now? Write down whatever comes to you, even if it is "Dear God, I don't know what to say." Even with such a beginning, choose to stay in that place for a while, and await what comes next.

---

2 For the sake of clarity, I have made very slight edits to what I originally wrote.

CHAPTER 6

Writing as a Spiritual Practice

What exactly does it look like to engage in writing as a spiritual practice? Does this mean writing takes a particular form, or has a different purpose? Some forms of writing are better suited than others. Journaling works well as a spiritual practice, as does poetry, but most forms of writing can work. Writing in the form of a prayer or psalm can be a creative way of adapting the third General Rule, which includes the practice of prayer as an instituted means of grace. What is most important is the intent of the writing. When my writing pays attention to God's movement in my life, it functions as a spiritual practice for me, moving me toward a deeper knowledge of myself and a closer relationship to God. Helen Cepero, who writes about journaling as a spiritual practice, aptly describes this twofold movement:

> The more authentically we travel into our own lives and our own stories, the more we will lay claim to God's image deep within us. This is both the beginning point and the destination. The more deeply we immerse ourselves in the story of God, the more our lives are filled with the love of Christ. . . . And the more available we are to God, the more available we are to truly love ourselves, one another and the world.[3]

Writing can help connect our inner world and the outer world, helping us see the continuity between who we have been and who we are now, and between what we say we believe and how we actually live.[4]

---

3   Helen Cepero, *Journaling as a Spiritual Practice: Encountering God Through Attentive Writing* (Downers Grove, IL: InterVarsity Press, 2008), 9.
4   Elizabeth J. Andrew, *Writing the Sacred Journey: The Art and Practice of Spiritual Memoir* (Boston: Skinner House, 2005), 5–6.

Writing as a spiritual practice requires me to tell the truth, or more specifically, my truth. Sometimes, opening myself to truth leads me to moments of clarity and insight, and a sense of being connected to myself and everything in creation as reflected in my journal entry at the beginning of this chapter. At other times, writing can reveal thoughts I'd rather not face, painful experiences I'd like to forget, or aspects about myself I'd prefer to ignore. I find this is especially the case with free writing, when I sit down with pen in hand with inchoate thoughts and swirling feelings and allow myself to write whatever comes to mind, ignoring grammar, spelling, and structure. Facing oneself honestly before God is not an easy thing to do at first, but doing so is a part of genuine spiritual practice, and it can be a source of healing.

More recently, much of my spiritual writing has taken the form of poems. Some of these poems make an explicit reference to God; some don't. Many of the poems I have written are about my experience of my mother's illness. Though I have written poetry on and off for much of my life, I returned to it more seriously when I realized that despite therapy earlier in my life, I still had a lot of unresolved grief related to my mother's illness and death. I thought I had come to terms with her death, but I realized that I had buried a lot of the pain related to my family's experience of living with her illness and being unable to talk to each other about our feelings.

Through poetry, I was able to access pain I had buried deeply and did not want to excavate, but knew was necessary for my healing and well-being. Most of the time I did not sit down saying to myself, "I'm going to write a poem." Rather, the words just take that form. The poem below was one I wrote not long after I started writing poetry more seriously as a part of a larger healing process, which also involved my return to therapy.

CHAPTER 6

White Dress

Graduation day
I pulled on the white dress and pumps
I picked out by myself.

A sunny day
like so many in Southern California,
the promise of pleasantness.

But the air turned foul,
in that room at the end of the hall
where you were confined to your bed.

I took off my white dress,
cleaned up the excrement of your illness
tried to wash away our embarrassment
wipe off the sorrow.

When I was done,
I slipped into my white dress,
picked up my cap and gown
and left without you.

I realize this may not be an easy poem to read. I find myself filled with sadness, and sometimes near tears when I read it—and I wrote it! I had occasionally shared with others that my mother had not been able to attend my high school graduation because of her illness, but I had not shared the details of that day, or the depth of my feelings about the experience. When I read these words, I revisit this pain, but I no longer carry it daily; it resides on the page. While there is no direct mention of God in this poem, releasing some of my pain through this poem allowed me to be more aware of God's presence in my life then and now. When my writing pays attention to God's movement in my life, it functions as a spiritual practice for me.

Unlike my journal entries, which I rarely reread and don't edit, I do edit my poems, though not always immediately after writing them. I want my poems to communicate as effectively as possible, and I do work on the craft of the poem, but I still don't consider myself a professional poet, or even a very good one. Perhaps I'll choose to publish my poems someday, but I don't write for that purpose. I do share my poems with a few select others to give voice to what had been silenced. Writing this poem marked a return to poetry and the beginning of a healing and transformative process.

When we allow writing to function as a spiritual practice, we may indeed find ourselves transformed. The writer and poet Pat Schneider reflects on her own transformation through writing as spiritual practice in evocative, artful language:

> Writing can be a spiritual practice. To write about what is painful is to begin the work of healing. To write the red of a tomato before it is mixed into beans for chili is a form of praise. To write an image of a child caught in war is confession or petition or requiem. To write grief onto a page of lined paper until tears blur the ink is often the surest access to giving or receiving forgiveness. To write a comic scene is grace and beatitude. To write irony is to seek justice. To write admission of failure is humility. To be in an attitude of praise or thanksgiving, to rage against God, or to open one's inner self and listen, is prayer. To write tragedy and allow comedy to arise between the lines is miracle and revelation. . . . Writing itself can open into mystery.[5]

---

5   Pat Schneider, *How the Light Gets In: Writing as a Spiritual Practice* (New York: Oxford University Press, 2013), 6–7.

This, I thought upon reading these words, *this is what I experience when I write*. I had never read words that so clearly and eloquently described my own experience. And as Schneider indicates, writing as a spiritual practice requires looking honestly into the depth of one's soul, which is not always an easy or pain-free process. Reading Schneider's words helped me realize that what I was doing in the poem "White Dress" was not just about releasing pain, but also about giving and receiving forgiveness. When we are willing to enter into the deep and sometimes painful places of our lives, we find God in those same places ready to move us toward healing and well-being. I believe such writing is a form of prayer in the sense that the purpose of prayer is to deepen the relationship between God and ourselves.

Exercise

Spiritual practices attune our attention to God in the ordinary. Schneider says writing opens us to mystery, and she begins with describing a tomato. Find something in your immediate environment, look at it, and write a detailed description of it using as many of your senses as you can. What do you see? If you can touch or pick up the object, how does it feel? Is there sound, smell, or taste associated with the object? (Maybe you have coffee in the cup you are contemplating.)

Writing as a Healing Practice

Writing is both a spiritual and healing practice for me. When we are stuck in emotional or physical pain, or coping with overwhelming stress, it can be hard for us to be attentive and aware of God's presence in our lives. Engaging in writing that heals can open up channels of grace that may be blocked by our own pain. Recently,

I have been revisiting my journals while writing this chapter and found an entry from January 1, 2016, that reflects on writing as a healing process. My entry begins with these words: "I am angry tonight and I don't know why." After listing possible reasons for my anger, I come to the realization that I am feeling the pangs of longing I often feel near the anniversary of my mother's death on January 3. I write:

> I feel this longing at this time of year, one that will never be filled. I miss my mother. I am still angry that I lost her too soon and that she suffered so much.
>
> All I want to do is write in my notebook. I no longer care what happens to these words—whether or not anyone reads them, still I want to put them down.
>
> Somehow, it feels like writing is a way of becoming real—putting the words somewhere. It doesn't matter if I have a witness. *It's the act of writing itself.*
>
> *I feel like I'm staking a claim.* (emphasis added)

A poem follows this journal entry in which I wonder if I have become too attached to my sorrow. The poem ends with these words: "Can I learn to wear my sorrow as a cloak, made of moonlight and shadows, light as breath?" I began my journal entry full of anger and sorrow, then realized I was doing something with my words, staking a claim to my experience, and leaving my anger on the page. Following the poem, I reflect on forgiveness, forgiving my mother for being ill, and myself for being a child, and merely human.

CHAPTER 6

The Healing Power of Expressive Writing

Poetry and journaling have been the primary ways that I have accessed the healing power of writing, but there are other methods of writing for healing that you might want to try. One well-researched method is expressive writing, developed by psychologist James W. Pennebaker.[6] For the last three decades, Pennebaker and his colleagues have conducted extensive research on "expressive writing," which has been shown to promote healing in the majority of participants.[7] Expressive writing is "a brief writing technique that helps people understand and deal with emotional upheavals in their lives."[8]

The method of expressive writing is rather simple: it involves writing for fifteen to twenty minutes a day over three to four days about difficult or traumatic experiences that you have not previously disclosed.[9] A central feature of expressive writing is reflecting on one's emotion related to the troublesome or traumatic event. Simply venting one's feeling about the event does not bring the same benefits.[10] Expressive writing seems to work best for dealing with something that has already happened or from which you have some distance, rather than when you are still in the thick of the trauma.[11] By helping us identify and process emotions and feelings about an experience, expressive writing can provide structure and

---

[6] James W. Pennebaker and John F. Evans, *Expressive Writing: Words That Heal* (Enumclaw, WA: Idyll Arbor, 2014), 3.
[7] Pennebaker and Evans, 3.
[8] James W. Pennebaker and Joshua M. Smyth, *Opening Up by Writing It Down: How Expressive Writing Improves Health and Eases Emotional Pain*, 3rd ed. (New York: Guilford Press, 2016), ix.
[9] Pennebaker and Smyth, 158–59.
[10] Pennebaker and Smyth, 21.
[11] Pennebaker and Smyth, 161.

order to confusing events, helping us make meaning out of a difficult experience.[12]

One need not focus on the most traumatic events of one's past, though one may decide to address these. Focusing one's writing on current issues can be helpful too.[13] What you write about is a personal decision. What is the issue or event that's bothering you—the one you can't seem to get out of your mind, and the more you push it away, the more it pops back up, demanding your attention? You may choose to write about a secret you have kept for some years, or you may choose to write about a conflict with a parishioner you don't feel free to share with anyone. Detailed directions for this process are found in Pennebaker's work.[14]

Pennebaker's extensive research shows that writing that includes confession or disclosure and that connects thoughts and feelings has more healing power than writing that simply dispassionately describes events.[15] Expressive writing draws on the power of personal disclosure (confession) to release us from the power of secrets and the damage they cause.[16] Keeping secrets, especially our own, can cause significant damage to our health, affecting our immune system, contributing to high blood pressure, and impairing emotional and mental health.[17] Holding back the "thoughts, feelings and behaviors" we deem secret can put us at risk for major and minor illnesses.[18] Inhibiting our thoughts and feelings, it turns out, takes considerable effort, which has both physical and

---

12 Pennebaker and Smyth, 78.
13 Pennebaker and Smyth, 167.
14 Pennebaker and Smyth, 167–70.
15 Pennebaker and Smyth, 1–2.
16 Pennebaker and Smyth, 1–2.
17 Pennebaker and Smyth, 10.
18 Pennebaker and Smyth, 10.

psychological consequences.[19] Disclosing a secret, he discovered, frees us from the effort and consequences of keeping it, and the result is often improved mental, physical, and spiritual health.[20]

I have not engaged in expressive writing in the form Pennebaker describes (fifteen minutes a day for three to four days), but I have engaged in journal and poetry writing that shares some of the same features. That is, the writing is confessional and links previously undisclosed thoughts and feelings around a difficult experience. These features can be seen in my journal entry earlier. I began by confessing my anger, though I was uncertain of its source, and in the process I discovered my longing and sadness, but the process of writing down what I felt led me to forgiveness and a sense of healing.

While I was in therapy in recent years, I wrote a poem titled "Dear Mom." I consider this a confessional poem in which I disclose something previously unsaid. Each stanza begins with words like "I never told you" or "I couldn't say." Three stanzas of the poem follow:

> I never told you how much I disliked
> having to feed you
> or that I tasted the Gerber strained peas
> and found them disgusting.
>
> I didn't say I wished you were like other mothers,
> able to shop with me for a dress
> for the prom.
>
> I couldn't tell you how frightened I was
> of your leaving me alone.

---

19 Pennebaker and Smyth, 10–11.
20 Pennebaker and Smyth, 11.

I shared this poem with my therapist because doing so provided the added benefit of a supportive, nonjudgmental listener. I have found that psychotherapy and forms of disclosive or confessional writing, like expressive writing, share similar goals of increasing self-awareness, and that they can be mutually supportive of each other.

In addition to my anecdotal evidence, scores of experimental studies by Pennebaker and his colleagues have produced evidence of the healing power of expressive writing. In one study, the researcher set out to discover if the expressive writing had any impact on the functioning of the immune system, which plays an important role in maintaining and restoring our physical health.[21] This experiment progressed as had many others: one group of volunteers wrote about a traumatic or difficult subject, without a prompt, while another group wrote about superficial topics, and all the volunteers agreed to have their blood drawn "the day before the writing session, after the last writing session, and six weeks later."[22] Volunteers disclosed a range of tragedies and traumatic events, from suicide, to various forms of abuse suffered, to family conflict.[23] The results revealed that those who "wrote about their deepest thoughts and feelings surrounding traumatic experiences evidence enhanced immune function," which was not the case for those who wrote about other topics.[24] The positive effect on the immune system of those who wrote about difficult events was greatest the day after the experiment, but persisted for the six weeks following.[25] The frequency of health visits dropped for those who wrote about trauma rather than trivial subjects.[26]

---

21 Pennebaker and Smyth, 20.
22 Pennebaker and Smyth, 20.
23 Pennebaker and Smyth, 20.
24 Pennebaker and Smyth, 21.
25 Pennebaker and Smyth, 21.
26 Pennebaker and Smyth, 21.

Expressive writing has some features that distinguish it from other forms of personal writing, such as journaling. First, one writes about a particular event or issue in short sessions over a period of several days. Second, one reflects on one's emotion related to the troublesome or traumatic event. Simply venting one's feelings about the event does not bring the same benefits, though our writing may begin there.[27] Expressive writing seems to work best for dealing with something that has already happened or from which you have some distance, rather than in the immediate aftermath of trauma.[28] By helping us identify and process emotions and feeling about an experience, expressive writing can provide structure and order to confusing events, helping us make meaning out of a difficult experience.[29]

Exercise

Identify an issue that has been bothering you that you have yet to disclose to anyone or can't disclose. Mark three to four days on your calendar in which you will try expressive writing. Explore the same topics over this time in fifteen- to twenty-minute segments.

Benefits of Confessional and Expressive Writing

Clergy are often put in a position of keeping secrets. We may carry our own secrets that we have never shared whose disclosure we fear may jeopardize our ministry. For example, I was sexually harassed by male church members in three different church settings early in my ministry. These encounters occurred after I had experienced a sexual assault by a former neighbor on a visit to his family while the rest of the family was out for the night. I

---

27 Pennebaker and Smyth, 21.
28 Pennebaker and Smyth, 161.
29 Pennebaker and Smyth, 78.

had tried to talk to a trusted aunt and her friend about what happened. Because my aunt responded with silence and her friend asked me, "What did you do to encourage him?" I never spoke of that event again, or of any other unwanted sexual advances, for fear I'd be asked that same question. I carried a lot of shame about all of these experiences for a long time. I kept not only my secret but also the secrets of those men who engaged in appropriate and unethical behavior.

We clergy are often put in the position of keeping other people's secrets as part of our pastoral responsibility. Perhaps you know a parishioner is terminally ill, but she has chosen not to share that information with her adult children or members of the congregation, despite your pleas to do so. Writing as a form of confession, of unburdening ourselves from secrets, can be included in a spiritual writing practice and may be beneficial to clergy burdened by their own secrets as well as the secrets of others. You might choose to use the specific technique of expressive writing, or you may find journaling or poetry writing more comfortable. Just writing it down can be helpful because it can help us stop ruminating, turning the same event or feeling over and over in our minds without resolution. The act of translating an image or phenomenon into writing changes the way it is represented in our minds.[30] The well-known saying "Confession is good for the soul" has truth in it. Confession has long been a spiritual practice in the church, though the formal practice of personal confession or even prayers of corporate confession have largely fallen out of favor. Clergy, however, are still the hearers and keepers of confession. Who will hear the confession of the clergy?

---

30 Pennebaker and Smyth, 145.

Exercise

Are you carrying a secret of yours or another's that is burdening you? Perhaps you know of a church member's affair, or an undisclosed illness. Perhaps a member of your staff left suddenly and you know why but can't share that information with the congregation. Write down your secret and reflect on how you feel doing so. You don't even have to keep a permanent record of what you write. You can destroy what you have written afterward if you are concerned it may be exposed.

More Benefits

While much of the research on expressive writing has involved the disclosure of traumatic events, it can be also used to work through less-severe problems, including family or church conflict, gaining clarity on a troublesome problem, or making a "life course correction."[31] I have often wondered if Barbara Brown Taylor kept a journal while she was trying to decide whether or not to leave her pulpit. It does seem to me that writing her memoir was a way to come to terms with a difficult period in her life. Perhaps she could not get the distance she needed on the events until after they occurred. Could she have gained clarity sooner if she had been writing about the events while they were occurring? Perhaps you simply write a pros and cons list on a sheet of paper while trying to make a difficult decision. Even that simple practice is a form of writing and can be helpful. Maybe you are trying to decide whether to stay at your current church or leave, or go back to school, or take a family leave. If you are undecided, write about it.

Expressive writing has also shown to be helpful in reducing the long-term stress of living with a chronic disease.[32] Since many of

---

31 Pennebaker and Smyth, 159–60.
32 Pennebaker and Smyth, 46.

the health concerns that plague clergy, such as high blood pressure or depression, are related to chronic conditions, expressive writing may reduce the stress of living with such conditions, leading to less stress on the immune system and improvements in health and overall well-being.[33] A consequence of the wellness syndrome is that we often feel responsible for our own well-being. When a chronic condition flares up, our inner critic may start scolding us. You can work through the steps of self-compassion in writing. Notice your pain, realizing that you are human and are not the only one struggling. Be kind to yourself. Write down advice you'd give to yourself as if you were talking to your best friend.

Writing is a reliable strategy in reducing the stress of those in caring professions.[34] Unlike therapists, clergy don't usually have extensive training in how to manage the burden of sharing in other people's pain or holding their secrets. Knowing that carrying confining stories shapes our caregiving in unhelpful ways can be a first step toward caring for the stories that make us who we are. Knowing the backstory of a church conflict or a parisioner's difficulty can help remind us that there are often bigger forces and stories at work in any situation.

Exercise

1) Are you facing a decision that you have been going around and around about, say, a job change, a move, or a change in relationship status? Try to describe the dilemma as clearly as you can, noting all the facets, all the possible options. Note not only your thoughts but your feelings about all of these possibilities.

2) Do you struggle with a chronic illness that flares up from time to time? Do you tend to blame yourself when this happens?

---

33 Pennebaker and Smyth, 59, 64.
34 Pennebaker and Smyth, 130.

Try writing through the steps of self-compassion listed in the previous section.

How to Begin Writing as a Spiritual Practice

How does one begin writing as a spiritual practice? If you have been engaging in the writing exercises throughout this book, you have already started. If you are already a writer, I hope you now have a fuller sense of how writing can fulfill the basic purpose of a spiritual practice: attending to God's presence and movement in our lives and in the world. Whatever your experience with writing, I find Pat Schneider's five "essential affirmations" that guide her writing workshops good advice for any writer wanting to write as a spiritual practice.[35]

1. Everyone has a strong unique voice.
2. Everyone is born with creative genius.
3. Writing as an art form belongs to all people, regardless of economic class or educational level.
4. The teaching of craft can be done without damage to a writer's original voice or artistic self-esteem. (This pertains to giving and receiving feedback on one's writing.)
5. A writer is someone who writes.[36]

Writing as a spiritual practice can take many different forms. Over the years, the form of my writing has changed. I see this when I look back through my journals. Some journal entries take a more traditional form of recording and reflecting on what's happening in my life. In other entries, I address God directly, asking for

---

35 Pat Schneider, *Writing Alone and with Others* (New York: Oxford University Press, 2003), xix.
36 Schneider, ix–x.

answers or some sign of divine presence. Sometimes my reflections take the form of a prayer or a psalm, which may express rejoicing, thanks, confession, petition, intercession, or lament. In more recent years, an increasing number of my journal entries are poems. In a scribbled entry from a workshop I attended with Pat Schneider, I wrote this: "Poetry is a spiritual practice for me—connecting me to myself, to God's promptings in my soul, and connecting to the soul of the world."[37] Whatever form our spiritual writing takes, it involves seeing God's activity in the world, the holy in the ordinary. Though many poets have done this better, I tried to capture this sense of seeing the ordinary things of life in a different way in the following poem:

Monroe Avenue

Five o'clock, at a red light on Monroe
Grady High School stadium squats silent
cars and harried drivers are forced to stop.
Concrete walls rise, lean over the sidewalk
a magnolia guarding a garbage bin
hides in its arms the fragrance of flowers.
I watch the light for a flicker of green, a flash
wings of a hawk glide to the top of the field light, perch
then, wings lift, on the fly, on the hunt,
the city presses in, cars surge forward.

A growing body of literature on writing as a spiritual practice is now available, and you can find any number of approaches, some of which I have introduced to you. Karen Hering has developed

---

[37] Karen Scheib, personal journal, 2013, writing retreat with Pat Schneider at Candler School of Theology, Emory University, Atlanta, GA.

a unique approach she calls "contemplative correspondence."[38] Her process is designed to be used in a congregational setting, though it can be adapted to small groups as well. Hering combines selected spiritual practices and writing methods intended to foster "sacred connection, spiritual growth, and creative flow."[39] When writing becomes a spiritual practice, it is "essentially receptive," as are other spiritual practices, like silent meditation or contemplative prayer, and is "meant for listening, opening, seeing, and apprehending."[40] Different from some forms of silent contemplation, however, the practice of "*scriptio divina* (holy or meditative writing)" uses words, like its sister and traditional practice, "*Lectio divina* (holy or meditative reading)."[41]

Each session focuses on a particular topic, such as hope or redemption.[42] The group leader guides the writers through four basic steps: (1) creating the space and time to write; (2) "welcoming [our] inner writer to the page"; (3) opening our senses to what is around us; (4) "engaging imagination and memory."[43] The process begins with *Lectio Divina* as the leader reads a written reflection, which may include scripture or poetry, then provides a related prompt for the writers. Several reflections and prompts may be given in a single session.

Using prompts to get one started in writing is a common strategy for groups and individual writers. I also find reading poetry helps lead me into my own reflective writing. This is especially true for me of poems that reflect the beauty of creation, or that point

---

38 Karen Hering, *Writing to Wake the Soul: Opening the Sacred Conversation Within* (New York: Atria Books, 2013), xx.
39 Hering, xx.
40 Hering, 22–23.
41 Hering, 22.
42 See Hering, chaps. 11 and 12 (145–74).
43 Hering, 44

me in some way to divine mystery, whether or not the language of the poem is overtly religious. Writing prompts can be found in any number of books on writing, such as Schneider's *Writing Alone and with Others*,[44] as well as those with a specific focus on writing as a spiritual practice, such as those by Helen Cepero and Elizabeth Jarrett Andrew. A line or two from a poem can make a good prompt. I'm fond of a couple of lines from an Emily Dickinson poem as a prompt on hope: "Hope is the thing with feathers/ That perches in the soul."[45] Psalms work equally well as a prompt, and you can follow the structure of a psalm to write your own.[46] For example, you might write the first line of Psalm 139, one of my favorites—"O LORD, you have searched me and known me" (v. 1)—and see where that leads you.

Writing as a spiritual practice has a number of advantages.

- It is inexpensive and requires few resources.
- It need not take much time.
- It is self-initiated and flexible. We can do it at the best time for us, in whatever time increments work for us.
- We can write only for ourselves, or we can choose to share our writing with others.
- Writing is portable.
- It is something we can do our entire lives, even when facing illness or difficulty.

---

44 Schneider, *Writing Alone and with Others*.
45 Emily Dickinson, "Hope Is the Thing with Feathers," Poets.org, accessed January 9, 2018, https://www.poets.org/poetsorg/poem/hope-thing-feathers-254.
46 See, for example, Ray McGinnis, *Writing Sacred Poetry: A Psalm-Inspired Path to Appreciating and Writing Sacred Poetry* (Kelowna, BC: Wood Lake Publishing, 2005).

- Writing as a spiritual practice requires no special gifts or inborn talent, though it does require a particular orientation and paying attention to the movement of the holy.[47]

Not every form of writing is a spiritual practice for me. Writing an academic article or a book review has a particular purpose. Writing as a spiritual practice is not about making an argument or having my say, but orienting and opening myself to the ground of being and the mystery of divine love. What distinguishes writing as a spiritual practice is less a matter of form than orientation and intention. Spiritual writing helps us attend to the "still small voice" (I Kings 19:12 NKJV) and provides "a way of listening to our inner truth and to the sacred source of that truth."[48]

Exercise

Pick a line of a favorite poem or psalm as a writing prompt. Write down that line and then free write for ten to fifteen minutes without stopping or worrying about spelling, grammar, or sentence structure.

Writing and Story Care

Story care begins with paying attention to our narratives. I can think of few better ways of doing this than through writing. Telling stories works too, but when we write our stories down, we can examine them in more detail. Writing is one of the primary ways we construct a narrative. Writing down thoughts, feelings, and experiences makes a story clearer. When an event has been

---

47 Helen DeSalvo, *Writing as a Way of Healing: How Telling Our Stories Transforms Our Lives* (Boston: Beacon Press, 2000), 13-15. I have adapted DeSalvo's list of reasons we write and the ways it can be a healing practice.

48 Hering, *Writing to Wake the Soul*, 28.

confusing or overwhelming, trying to construct a narrative out of it may seem difficult at first, but the very act of doing so can bring some organization to a confusing whirl of events, thoughts, and feelings.[49] Good life stories have some sense of coherence; that is, they make sense and are not closed off, but are open to further development and allow for some ambiguity.[50] A good life story has some resonance with the reality of our own lives, and is not lost in fantasy.[51] A good story has complexity, or thickness. I'm not sure if my poem "White Dress" is a good poem, but it is a pretty good story. Writing it helped me make sense out of a lot of confusing feelings I had tucked away for a very long time. Even though the poem is quite brief, it is coherent—you can follow the story. While the poem ends, it is clear the story hasn't ended. In that sense it is open, since we don't really know what happens next. The poem is simple, but the emotions in it are quite complex: love, sadness, embarrassment, a sense of loss, shame, and tender caring.

Once we begin paying closer attention to our stories and reading them more closely, we begin to see where our narratives may be confining us, where we are being influenced by a backstory we did not know, or recognize an under-told or untold story. These assessments may help us know when we need to engage in more intentional restorying.

A few years ago, my restorying process was prompted by the arrival of a box in the mail from my stepsister, which arrived about a year after my father's death. The family home was being sold, and my stepsister was kind enough to send me some things that had belonged to my mother. By then my mother had been dead for about twenty-five years. I found things in the box I had completely

---

49 Pennebaker and Smyth, *Opening Up by Writing It Down*, 152.
50 Scheib, *Pastoral Care*, 117 (see chap. 1, n. 2).
51 Scheib, 117.

forgotten about: a plate from the church where my parents were married, my father's small Bible, and some of my mother's writing. I avoided reading her writing for several months, wondering if I would be invading her privacy. When I did finally start reading through her work, I found a piece she had written describing the day she received her diagnosis after at least two years of unexplained symptoms. Reading her words inspired the following poem.

Yellowed Pages

A box arrived in the mail
unexpected gift, miscellaneous memories
yellowed typed pages, my mother's words
recovered.

A scene takes form, a cold exam table
two letters spoken in a doctor's sonorous voice,
mysterious symptoms named
MS.

I find myself fourteen, trying to button pajamas,
you keep falling over, you tell me,
a round-bottomed doll, you say.
We laugh.

I had forgotten this sweet beginning.

Reading my mother's reflections, then writing about it in this poem as well as in my journal, I realized two things: First, in constructing my story of my mother's illness, I had focused primarily on my experience, which makes sense. I was still a teenager when all this happened, with limited abilities to process all that was going on. But as an adult looking back, I realized I had a rather constricted story of this time in my life. Second, I had simply forgotten a lot of things that might have helped me construct a more open and complex story. I had not thought about my mother as a writer in a very long time. Pulling out some of the pages, I recognized notes written by her writing teacher, and I remembered having gone to a writing class with her. My primary memories of my mother had been so tinted by her illness that other dimensions of her life had faded. I had a sepia-toned image of her. I had forgotten the colors of her life, her imagination, her desires, her creativity. I had seen my mother only as my mother, not as a whole person with her own hopes, dreams, and sorrows. I started to get curious about who my mother was before she was my mother, and asked her only remaining sister about her memories of my mother as a girl and young woman. I did not get as much information as I would have liked, but I got enough to realize my mother had a much larger backstory than I had known.

Restorying this significant part of my life did not happen simply through writing one poem. It was a long, and sometimes difficult, process. As I began to revise my personal story, my story of myself as a pastor and pastoral care provider was also restoried. I gained a greater sense of freedom to care *for* others without feeling responsible for taking care *of* them. While I knew there had been much pain in that period of my life, I was able to see more clearly that there had been much love too. As I read those yellowed pages, I could see my mother's tenderness and care for me as well as mine for her. Remembering the tender moments is still painful, even as I write these words, because it reminds me of my longing and my loss. It was as if my memory were clouded with sorrow and I could remember only that. Once that cloud began to lift by writing into and through the darkness, I could see more clearly that I had loved well and was well loved, and am well loved. While writing played an important part in my new awareness, I could not have arrived where I am now without faithful story companions. We tell a story to someone; this someone may be God, who hears our stories uttered in prayer, or written out on the page, or it may be a friend, pastor, professional counselor, or spiritual director.

Story Care and Pastoral Identity (Reprise)

Through tending our stories we can arrive at a renewed understanding of both our personal and pastoral identity. I now feel I am living my call in a way that does not jeopardize my own well-being, which I have discovered allows me to be more attentive to the well-being of others. I have arrived at this point in my life by learning to attend to my story, including parts I would rather ignore, including my need to care for others in order to feel worthy of love. Learning to attend to my own story, to care for it, has allowed me to see more clearly how my story is connected to others' stories, and God's story. For me, the result has been a transformed sense of personal and pastoral identity. I now feel greater freedom in caring for others and a deep sense of fulfillment, which are at the heart of happiness. Flourishing is, of course, less a destination than a journey, and rarely a direct route. I have invited you to enter into this journey, to attend to your story through the various exercises in this book. My hope is that by attending to your story, you will find new ways of caring for yourself while caring for others. My sincere desire is that doing so leads to growth in love toward the flourishing God intends.

CPSIA information can be obtained
at www.ICGtesting.com
Printed in the USA
LVHW020721131118
596892LV00004B/6